ALL THE BEST RICE

D0118282

ALL THE BEST

RICE

BY
JOIE WARNER

HEARST BOOKS • **New York**

A FLAVOR BOOK

Copyright © 1994 by Flavor Publications

All rights reserved. No part of this book may be
reproduced or utilized in any form or by any means,
electronic or mechanical, including photocopying,
recording or by any information storage and retrieval
system, without permission in writing from the
copyright holder or the Publisher. Inquiries should be
addressed to Permissions Department, William Morrow
and Company, Inc. 1350 Avenue of the Americas,
New York, New York 10019

Recognizing the importance of preserving what has
been written, it is the policy of William Morrow and
Company, Inc., and its imprints and affiliates to have
the books it publishes printed on acid-free paper, and
we exert our best efforts to that end.

LIBRARY OF CONGRESS CATALOGING-IN-PUBLICATION DATA
Warner, Joie.
    All the best rice/by Joie Warner.
        p.   cm.
Includes index.
ISBN 0-688-13345-2
1. Cookery (Rice)   I. Title.
TX809.R5W37   1994
641.6'318 -- dc20   94-19234
                                              CIP

Printed in the United States of America
10 9 8 7 6 5 4 3 2 1

This book was created and produced by

Flavor Publications, Inc.
208 East 51st Street, Suite 240
New York, New York 10022

ACKNOWLEDGMENTS

THANKS TO Sarah Best, Susan Allen, Debbie Fine, Amy Lee, Maura Segal, Louise and Thom Northrop, Paul Paganelli, Sharee Fiore, Kathleen Johnson, Annie Hogan, Marcia Lowther, Susan Grant, Margaret Jackson – and Miss Penny – who loves rice, too.

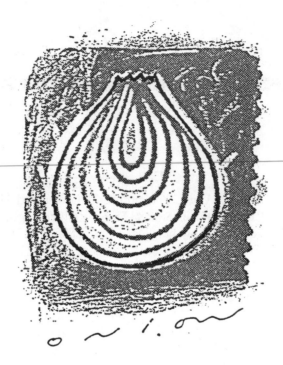

onion

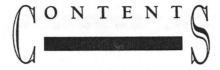CONTENTS

INTRODUCTION

RICE IS NOT NEW in America: what is new is its new-found popularity. Long relegated to the back reaches of the cupboard, rice is finally coming into its own. But rice is quite old. In fact, rice was cultivated in America long before the Civil War in the Carolinas. But the rice industry there eventually faltered and it gradually became established in Louisiana and then spread to other southern states.

Of course, there's old and then there's old. In Asia, rice has been around for a very long time – maybe as long as 7,000 years – and the Chinese were the first to domesticate rice, cultivating it in man-made paddies.

For many people from many cultures on many continents, rice is the staff of life. In China, rice is so essential to life that they have a saying, "a meal without rice is like a beautiful woman with only one eye." The Chinese greet each other with "have you eaten rice today?" and the word for rice is the same as that for food. Chinese children are told that for every grain of rice left in their bowl, there will be a pockmark on the face of their future spouse.

Today in the United States, over ninety percent of rice is grown in Louisiana and the southwest – Texas and California. I'll bet few know – it was news to me – that fifty percent of the crop is exported – some even to Japan – and that the U.S. is the second-largest exporter of rice in the world.

That may change as we experiment more and more with different cuisines, learn to appreciate the versatility, and, in these health-conscious times, discover the high nutritive value of rice. Did you know that rice has four times the food value of potatoes or pasta? Food for thought!

From a health standpoint, brown rice, with the husk and bran intact, provides the highest energy punch, but white rice is also healthful and wholesome, containing only a trace of fat and salt, very few calories and no cholesterol. As well, rice is high in complex carbohydrates and nutrients and is also nonallergenic and gluten-free. While rice does not contain every essential nutrient, when it's paired with small nuggets of fish, chicken, vegetables, or beans – as it is in many cultures around the globe – it becomes a nutritionally balanced meal.

Nowadays, most domestically grown white rice is enriched with vitamins and minerals, particularly thiamin, niacin, and iron. That's why it's important not to rinse domestic polished white rice before you cook it, and why it's better to have the rice absorb all the water or liquid it's cooked in to retain those added nutrients.

Just as we learned there's more to pasta than spaghetti, so, too, we are starting to discover the myriad varieties of rice which, depending on who you consult, number between seven thousand and forty thousand!

First, there's long-grain, medium-grain, and short-grain rice, each with its advocates, each best suited to different dishes. In America, most of the rice we eat is long-grain. That's because Americans tend to prefer a rice whose grains cook up separate, light, and fluffy. Long-grain rice is also the first choice in India, Southeast Asia, Mexico, and parts of the Middle East and China.

Short-grain rice sticks together when cooked, making it easy to eat with chopsticks, and this is the kind you'll find in Japanese dishes, especially sushi. Around the Mediterranean, short-grain rice, such as the Arborio variety from Italy, or the Valencia variety from Spain, is preferred and is essential in creating creamy risotto or colorful paella, pilau, and pilaf. Fat, oval, sticky rice – known as glutinous or sweet rice – is appreciated in parts of China and is popular for making dim sum such as *normaigai* (sticky rice in lotus leaves), pearl balls (rice-covered pork meatballs), and desserts.

In the supermarket, we mostly find white, long-grain rice and packaged rice that is parboiled or "converted." Brown rice and wild rice are also readily available.

Then there are the increasingly popular aromatics (rice with an alluring aroma), including Basmati from India, Jasmine rice from Thailand, and home-grown varieties such as Texmati, Konriko Wild Pecan, and Wahini, that you can find in some supermarkets or at specialty stores.

Whatever your choice, rice is readily available and inexpensive and is easy to keep on hand. Even the most exotic varieties are economical: two cups of raw rice will easily serve six.

And rice is so versatile and easy to cook: you can steam it, boil it, bake it, microwave it; you can prepare it in any old pan, a steamer, the latest microwave or electric rice cooker, or bake it pilaf-style in the oven. I recommend you make up a big batch because it's more difficult to get perfect results with a very small quantity and because it's so easy to use the leftovers.

In the recipes that follow, you'll find rice as an appetizer, a soup, a main meal, as a side dish, and for dessert. If you haven't yet tried rice flour, rice noodles, or rice paper, you have a few treats coming. Rice also makes a very palatable wine, as those who have tried saki can attest, but it's difficult to find a simple, do-it-yourself recipe!

I have always raved over rice – many of my favorite entrées are those married with or accompanied by the glorious grain. And – though it may sound a little peculiar – a simple bowl of rice with a drizzle of soy sauce is one of my favorite snacks. Yes, I like rice so much that my Chinese friends tell me I'm more Chinese than they are! But I love rice in all its guises and nationalities. And I can't wait to share with you many of my favorite dishes. Wait till you try Risotto with Sweet Italian Sausage and Tomato, or Spicy Seafood Gumbo, or Wild Rice and Mushroom Soup, or Pesto and Pecan Rice. This eclectic collection would not be complete without my favorite rice pudding recipe – citrus-scented, of course!

I've usually indicated the variety of rice I prefer, but in most (but not all) cases you are free to substitute your own favorite, as long as you match the grain type (long, medium, or short) as this is important to the look, texture, and taste of the dish.

On the following pages, you'll find more detailed information about the different varieties of rice and hints on the various ways of cooking them for best results.

I hope through these recipes you and your family will enjoy discovering new taste sensations as you add rice dishes to your repertoire of everyday favorites – I know I'm still amazed at just how versatile rice really is. So, go rescue that rice from the back reaches of the cupboard and discover the treasures you have in store!

JOIE WARNER

♦ ♦ ♦

BASICS

CHOOSING RICE

First there's size and shape, then there's color, and then there's the question of age – but let's not get carried away – it's really quite easy to find your way through the choices available.

You need to be able to distinguish the three basic types: long-grain, medium-grain, and short-grain rice. Long-grain (white and brown) rice is at least three times as long as it is wide and the grains cook up fluffy and remain separate. Medium-grain rice is shorter and more rounded than long-grain and the grains have a tendency to stick together when cooked. Short-grain rice is oval-shaped and is the most glutinous, that is, the cooked grains are very sticky.

Most rice produced in the United States is regular milled white (also called polished), long-grain rice that has been "enriched" with minerals and vitamins to compensate for the husk and bran layers of the grain being removed in the milling process. Parboiled or "converted" white rice has been steam-cooked before milling which retains more nutrients than regular long-grain. But it also requires more water and takes somewhat longer to cook. Also, parboiled rice is firmer and stays more separate than other varieties. The precooked and instant varieties have already been cooked and dehydrated for fast preparation. But since they lack both flavor and texture, the quick five-minute cooking is – in the end – a waste of time as well as money.

Brown rice has simply had the husk removed with the bran layers still intact. The bran is what gives the rice its brown color, chewy texture, and nutty taste. It has more fiber and slightly more nutrients than polished white.

You can now find a large selection of the more exotic varieties of what are called aromatics, both domestic and imported. Easiest to find is Basmati, a sweetly aromatic long-grain rice from India and Pakistan that is aged up to two years in order to increase its fragrance. Just like fine wines – the older the rice, the better – and the more expensive. Basmati is the only rice that elongates when cooked – nearly doubling in length – rather than expanding in width as other rices do. Another favorite of mine is Jasmine, also called scented rice, which has the faint aroma of jasmine. Imported from Thailand, it is superb with stir-fry dishes.

There are many aromatic hybrids now being cultivated in the U.S. For example, there's Watami, a brown rice with a Basmati-like fragrance; Texmati, which is also similar to Basmati with a nutty flavor; a Wild Pecan Rice called Konriko from Louisiana that isn't really a wild rice and has a slight pecan flavor; and Lundberg Wahani and Black Japonica rice from California. All are long-grain – except Black Japonica which is a short-grain rice – and can generally be used interchangeably in most recipes.

The Arborio, Vialone Nano, and Canaroli varieties from Northern Italy are the shortest and roundest of the short-grain varieties and contain just the right amount of starch for creating the creamiest risotto imaginable. Another short-grain rice to be on the look out for is Valencia from Spain and it is worth finding to make a truly outstanding paella.

Botanically, wild rice is not a true rice but a seed of an aquatic grass that grows wild in the Great Lakes region of Canada and the U.S.

White rice will keep for a fairly long time – ideally in a well-sealed, airtight container kept in a cool, dark cupboard. I buy my rice in sacks because I use so much, but I take great care where I buy it and how I store it since it can attract insects.

Because of the oil in the bran layers, brown rice does not keep well – it begins to turn rancid after a few months. I recommend you buy just the quantity you need when you need it. Some cooks keep it in the refrigerator to keep it fresher longer. Wild rice will keep indefinitely in a tightly covered container in a cool, dry cupboard.

Have rice at the ready and you'll always have the makings of a quick-and-simple, spur-of-the-moment dinner.

COOKING RICE

Rice is one of the simplest foods to cook, yet one of the easiest to spoil by overcooking.

For most people, allow a half-cup of raw rice per person when the rice is an accompaniment to a stew such as a beef bourguignon or a curry, or is being served with a stir-fry. If you are a rice lover, like me, double the amount. And since it is more difficult to get good results when using very small quantities, I usually cook at least two cups of raw rice and save any leftovers for another time. It is very easy to reheat cooked rice, especially if you have a microwave, or to add milk, cream, and sugar and bake it into rice pudding, or to make fried rice the next time you fancy a fast, Chinese-style supper.

I wish I could give you an exact rice-to-water ratio that would give perfect results every time, but there are just too many variables – the age of the rice (older takes more water), the variety (brown takes longer and takes more water), the size and shape of the saucepan – and the cooking method chosen. At least, though, I can share with you my simple secrets to success.

1. Rinse rice thoroughly if you buy it in bulk or if it is imported.
2. Do not rinse domestic polished rice that has been "enriched" with added nutrients and never rinse Italian Arborio rice. The starch is necessary for making creamy risotto.
3. For dry, fluffy rice, I use an electric rice cooker or a heavy 2½-quart saucepan (see Equipment) for cooking 1 to 2 cups long-grain rice. If grains are too firm, add ¼ cup more water next time.
4. Do not stir rice unless the recipe instructs you to do so, except once to combine the salt with the water and rice. Stirring rice mashes the grains which allows the starch to escape, causing gummy rice.
5. Cover the pan in which you are cooking the rice with a good, tight-fitting lid.
6. Cook rice over medium-low heat – not too low, or the rice cooks too long and becomes sticky.
7. If rice is too firm, add a little more water, cover, and continue cooking until tender. If rice is too moist, remove cover, fluff with a fork, and continue cooking, uncovered, until moisture has evaporated.

8. Once the rice is done, remove the pan from the heat, uncover, and let stand for 5 minutes to dry the rice a little before serving.
9. To reheat leftover rice, break up any lumps, add to saucepan (or heatpoof bowl if microwaving) and sprinkle some water over the top. Cover, if cooking in a saucepan, and reheat over low heat. I don't cover rice if reheating in a microwave and I reheat it on high for a minute or so.

METHODS

Rice can be cooked in a heavy saucepan on top of the stove, in an electric rice cooker, or baked in the oven.

RICE COOKERS: I cook a lot of rice and find an automatic rice cooker indispensable. Besides supplementing the stove, it's absolutely foolproof. The rice is placed in the container with water added to about 1 inch above its surface – don't follow the manufacturer's instructions for the amount of water to add – use the proportions in the following recipes – then it's covered and switched on. That's all there is to it. No need to watch the pot – it shuts off automatically when done and keeps the rice warm until serving time.

BOILING WATER METHOD: Some cooks – and many restaurants – use the "boiling water method." A large pot of water is brought to a boil over high heat, rice is added and it's cooked like pasta until tender – you have to keep tasting to test doneness, then the excess water is drained in a colander. Nutrients are drained away, too, so it's not really the best method.

COVERED SAUCEPAN METHOD: Most cooks use this method. Rice, water, and salt are put in a heavy, covered saucepan and brought to a boil. The pan is then covered, the heat reduced to medium-low, and the rice cooked for 15 to 20 minutes or until the water is absorbed and the rice is tender.

MICROWAVE: I only use the microwave for reheating rice. However, it can be useful if you want to cook just a very small quantity. Combine ½ cup rice with 1 cup water in a 4-cup glass measuring cup. Microwave on medium power for 12 minutes, turning dish a couple of times. Check. When rice has absorbed nearly all the water, remove dish, cover, and let stand for 5 minutes before fluffing and serving.

You may have to adjust power and cooking time depending on the wattage of your microwave.

STEAMING: This method is used for glutinous rice. Soak the rice for several hours or overnight before steaming to provide enough moisture and reduce the cooking time. Place the rice in a steamer basket over a large pot or wok of gently boiling water and steam for 20 minutes or until tender.

BAKED METHOD: The rice, water, and salt (in the same proportions as for simmered rice) are added to a casserole or enameled or glass baking dish, covered, and baked in a preheated 400°F oven for 25 minutes or until tender.

EQUIPMENT

CHOPSTICKS: Even the most maladroit Westerner can get the knack of scooping up rice with a little practice, and chopsticks are also useful as kitchen tools for mixing, beating, stirring, lifting or turning food, especially when stir-frying. *The* perfect tool for fluffing rice.

ELECTRIC RICE COOKERS: For those who cook a lot of rice, these are ideal. These counter-top appliances are easy to use and can be left unattended. Don't follow the manufacturer's instructions for the amount of water to add – use the proportions in the following recipes. Rice cookers are available in Chinatown, many department stores, and specialty cookware shops.

HEAVY SAUCEPAN: A heavy saucepan with a tight-fitting lid is essential. I use a 2½-quart Calphalon saucepan for 1 to 2 cups rice although a 2-quart saucepan is sufficient.

STORAGE CONTAINERS: Glass or plastic storage containers with tight-fitting covers are perfect for storing rice. I buy several varieties of rice – wild, Basmati, Jasmine, regular long-grain, etc. – in very large quantities and store them carefully.

INGREDIENTS

ANDOUILLE SAUSAGE: A smoked Cajun pork sausage. Kielbasa sausage may be substituted.

ARBORIO RICE: A short-grain rice from Northern Italy that is traditionally used for risotto. It is readily available at many supermarkets or at Italian food markets.

ARTICHOKES, MARINATED: Artichoke hearts are prepared with oil and herbs and bottled. You can find them at most supermarkets or in specialty food stores. Look for greenish rather than grayish ones.

BASMATI RICE: A delicately scented, long-grain rice from India that is available at health food or specialty stores, some supermarkets, and from Asian markets It should be thoroughly rinsed before using.

BLACK OLIVES: I use Kalamata olives from Greece which are available at the deli counter or from specialty food stores. You may also use Niçoise olives from France. Canned American olives do not have the flavor and pungency called for in these recipes.

BLACK PEPPER: I always use freshly ground black peppercorns.

BROWN RICE: Brown rice takes longer to cook and has more texture than white and it has a more earthy taste. It is readily available in most supermarkets.

CAMBOZOLA: A creamy-textured, mild blue cheese from Germany.

CAPERS: These are the unopened flower buds of a Mediterranean shrub. You can find the tiny French capers or larger, Spanish ones. They are packed in vinegar (not salt), and I never rinse them.

CARIBBEAN HOT SAUCE: An extraordinarily hot, distinctively flavored chile sauce made from the hottest pepper in the world – the habanero – also know as Scotch bonnet peppers. Use the red-colored sauce – not the yellow. Available in some supermarkets and Caribbean markets.

CHÈVRE: A fresh, soft, mild-tasting cheese made from goat's milk that can be found in supermarkets or in well-stocked cheese shops.

CHINESE BARBECUED PORK: A sweet-tasting glazed pork available in Chinese barbecue shops – the ones with meats and poultry hanging in the window.

CHINESE DRIED BLACK MUSHROOMS: Dried mushrooms that are sold in cellophane bags and clear plastic boxes in Chinese markets. They last indefinitely in a covered container. They must be reconstituted in hot water for 30 minutes before using.

CHINESE SAUSAGE: Pink-colored, sweet tasting pork sausages that are sold in shrink-wrap packages in the refrigerator section in Chinese markets. They must be steamed for about 15 minutes before eating. Sausages will keep for months in the freezer.

CILANTRO: A pungent herb also known as coriander or Chinese parsley.

CURRY POWDER: The best curry powder is found in East Indian markets.

FETA CHEESE: A firm white, slightly salty cheese from Greece. You can find it at the deli counter, in well-stocked cheese shops and at Greek food stores.

GARLIC: You'll find garlic in nearly all my recipes for it is a seasoning that goes with almost every savory dish. Choose large bulbs that are tightly closed and not sprouting. Squeeze the bulb to make sure it is firm and fresh. Avoid powdered garlic.

GINGER: Always use fresh ginger. Powdered ginger and fresh ginger are not interchangeable. Select young ginger with a smooth, shiny skin. It will last for months in the refrigerator if first wrapped in a paper towel, then placed in a plastic bag. The paper towel must be replaced often or it will become moldy.

GLUTINOUS RICE: or "sweet" rice, sticks together when cooked.

GORGONZOLA: A very creamy, mold-ripened cheese from Lombardy in Italy. It is available in Italian food shops or well-stocked cheese stores.

HOT PEPPER RINGS: These bottled pickled sliced peppers – usually red, green, and yellow – are available in the pickle section of most supermarkets.

JALAPEÑOS: These recipes call for the readily available canned pickled sliced chiles, which can be found in the Mexican food section of most supermarkets.

JASMINE RICE: A long-grain rice, also known as Thai scented rice because of its delicate scent. It can be found in health and specialty stores and in Asian markets.

KIELBASA SAUSAGE: A smoked Polish sausage available in quality butcher shops and at some supermarket deli counters. Avoid the packaged variety.

LEEKS: To clean, slice leek in half lengthwise, leaving root intact. Place under cold, running water, fanning the sections as necessary to remove sand. Drain well.

LEMON GRASS: A Thai herb of tall, slim green reeds. The pale-colored part of the stalk is used. It's available in Asian markets and some supermarkets. Avoid the powdered and dried forms.

LONG-GRAIN WHITE RICE: The most commonly found rice on supermarket shelves; look for regular rice (not precooked or instant). Do not rinse domestic rice before using or you will lose the added nutrients.

MASCARPONE: Similar to cream cheese, but sweeter and creamier and more delicately flavored. It can be found in Italian food shops or well-stocked cheese stores.

MONTEREY JACK: Sort of a cross between Cheddar and mozzarella cheese with excellent melting qualities. It's available in most supermarkets and well-stocked cheese shops.

MOZZARELLA: Renowned for its perfect melting qualities, the brand I purchase is shrink-wrapped in the shape of a ball about the size of an orange. The familiar part-skim mozzarella found in supermarkets tends to be bland and rubbery.

MUSTARD: Grainy mustards are coarse in texture and very aromatic. Dijon mustard has a smooth texture and well-rounded flavor. Both can be found in most supermarkets.

NUTMEG: Purchase whole nutmegs and grate just before using for best flavor.

OKRA: This tropical plant native to Africa is either loved or detested because of its slippery texture. It helps thicken stews and is often found in Southern U.S. recipes. I use the frozen (not canned) variety in these recipes which is readily available at most supermarkets.

OLIVE OIL: I prefer to use an extra-virgin, cold-pressed oil with a delicate olive taste.

PANCETTA: An Italian-style bacon that is unsmoked, seasoned with pepper and spices then rolled. You can find it at the deli counter or Italian food markets.

PARMESAN: Be sure to purchase Parmesan that has the words "Parmigiano Reggiano" or, second best, "Grana Padano" stamped on the rind. Always grate it fresh just before using because it begins to lose flavor after grating. It is available in Italian food shops or well-stocked cheese stores.

PROSCIUTTO: This salted, air-dried Italian ham is available in Italian food shops and at some supermarket deli counters.

RICE PAPER WRAPPERS: Paper-thin, round or triangular-shaped wrappers that are transparent and pliable when softened in water. They are available in Asian markets.

RICE STICK NOODLES: Very fine noodles made from rice, they are called rice sticks or rice vermicelli. They are available in Asian markets.

ROASTED RED PEPPERS: Peppers that are roasted or broiled until the skin blackens, then peeled and seeded. Fresh-made are best, but you may substitute the bottled variety They are available in supermarkets and Italian markets.

ROMANO CHEESE: A hard grating sheep's milk cheese similar to Parmesan, but stronger in flavor. The best is known as "pecorino" and it's available in quality cheese shops and Italian markets. Avoid the pre-grated kind on the supermarket shelf.

STRAW MUSHROOMS (CANNED): So named because they are grown on beds of rice straw. Available in Asian grocers and some supermarkets.

SUN-DRIED TOMATOES: These have become very popular in the past few years and can be found almost everywhere. Avoid brownish-colored ones.

THAI COCONUT MILK: The liquid is obtained from pressing the coconut flesh, not the liquid found inside the coconut. I use the unsweetened canned coconut milk, not the sweetened coconut cream for drinks! The best coconut milk comes from Thailand. Stir it well before using; the cream tends to rise to the top. The brand I use has a picture of a measuring cup and a coconut on the label. It's available in Asian food stores and some supermarkets.

THAI FISH SAUCE: The Thai name for this fermented fish sauce is *nam pla* (in Vietnam it's called *nuoc nam*). It is used as a condiment and seasoning ingredient in Southeast Asian cooking. A good quality fish sauce is Squid Brand from Thailand. It's available in Asian food shops and some supermarkets.

THAI GREEN CURRY PASTE: Available in Asian markets, it is similar to red curry paste except it contains green chiles and cilantro.

THAI RED CURRY PASTE: Available in Asian markets, red curry paste is a hot-and-spicy mixture of red chilies, garlic, ginger, coriander, turmeric, lemongrass and other seasonings. Curry powder is not a substitute for curry paste.

TOMATOES, FRESH: Use only flavorful, ripe, unwaxed tomatoes. If not fully ripe when you purchase them, allow them to ripen at room temperature. I never refrigerate tomatoes: the cold takes away their taste. When not available, substitute cherry or plum tomatoes which are flavorful all year long.

TORTA DI GORGONZOLA: A cheese made by layering Gorgonzola and mascarpone cheese. It is available in Italian food shops or well-stocked cheese stores.

VERMOUTH: I like to use French dry white vermouth in my recipes instead of dry white wine since it keeps better.

APPETIZERS

♦ ♦ ♦

CHINESE PEARL BALLS

Delicate dim sum *pork meatballs are rolled in pearly sweet glutinous rice and steamed until the rice coating* becomes beautifully translucent and shiny – the color of pearls – hence the name. ◆ *The rice is first soaked, to soften before steaming, and once the meatballs have been coated, they must be steamed right away or the rice will dry out. The meatballs can be resteamed once more without too much loss of flavor.*

1 pound ground pork
1 large egg
6 Chinese dried black mushrooms, soaked for 30 minutes in hot water, squeezed dry, stems discarded, diced
2 whole green onions, finely chopped
6 fresh or canned water chestnuts, chopped
1 tablespoon sugar
1 tablespoon soy sauce
1 tablespoon dry sherry

1 tablespoon Japanese sesame oil
½ teaspoon salt
1 cup sweet (glutinous) rice, rinsed, soaked for 4 hours in water to cover
2 tablespoons soy sauce
1 tablespoon red wine vinegar
1 teaspoon Japanese sesame oil
¼ teaspoon sugar
1 small garlic clove, finely chopped

COMBINE PORK, egg, mushrooms, green onions, water chestnuts, 1 tablespoon sugar, 1 tablespoon soy sauce, dry sherry, 1 tablespoon sesame oil, and salt in medium bowl.

Drain rice; spread out on tray. Form pork mixture into meatballs, using about a heaping tablespoon for each. Roll meatballs in rice, making sure they are completely coated.

Place rack in wok; fill wok with water to bottom edge of rack, and place glass pie plate on rack. Cover; bring to a boil.

Using tongs, place meatballs about ½ inch apart (do in 3 batches) on pie plate, cover, and steam for 15 minutes over high heat or until cooked through. Don't overcook; keep warm. Steam remaining meatballs in same manner. Meanwhile, combine 2 tablespoons soy sauce, red wine vinegar, 1 teaspoon sesame oil, sugar, and garlic in small bowl; set dipping sauce aside. Serve pearl balls on warm platter with dip. Serves 4 to 6.

RICE-PAPER SPRING ROLLS

¼ cup water
¼ cup rice vinegar
¼ cup sugar
2 tablespoons Thai fish
  sauce
1 teaspoon hot red pepper
  flakes
¼ cup shredded carrot
1 garlic clove, minced
4 ounces rice-stick noodles,
  soaked for 10 minutes
  in hot water, drained
12 round (8½-inch)
  rice-paper wrappers

½ teaspoon sugar
1 tablespoon fresh lime
  juice
1 tablespoon Thai fish
  sauce
¾ pound cooked small
  (salad) shrimp
2 medium carrots, coarsely
  shredded
About ½ cup fresh cilantro
  or basil leaves
About ½ cup fresh mint
  leaves
Several lettuce leaves,
  coarsely shredded

COMBINE FIRST 7 ingredients in small serving bowl; set dipping sauce aside. Blanch drained noodles in boiling water for 1 minute, drain, and cool. Using scissors, cut noodles into 2-inch pieces, discarding tough clumps.

Fill large bowl with warm water. Dip rice paper wrappers in water; place in single layer on clean dish towels and wait several seconds until softened.

Stir sugar, lime juice, and fish sauce in large bowl until blended; add shrimp, carrots, and noodles and combine. Divide mixture evenly, placing on bottom third of each wrapper. Top with whole cilantro and mint leaves and several shreds of lettuce. Roll wrapper around filling, tucking in sides, until closed. (Try first roll, then adjust herbs and lettuce to taste.) Press to seal and place seam side down on lettuce-lined platter. Serve with dipping sauce. Makes 12 rolls.

*T*hese fantastic, fresh-tasting Thai bundles are not deep-fried, are low in fat, and they're loaded with rice noodles, crunchy carrots, and shrimp. (Substitute crabmeat if desired.) The sweet-and-spicy dip tops them off sublimely. ◆ The rolls and dipping sauce can be made several hours in advance, covered with plastic wrap and refrigerated. ◆ Miniature, cocktail-size nibbles are easily made by using smaller rice paper wrappers.

Black
Peppercorns

Pepper
mill

SOUPS

◆ ◆ ◆

E at your broccoli! It's good for you! Mother was right all along and this is as good a way as any to enjoy this nutritious – and I think delicious – vegetable. ♦ For a simple, satisfying supper, serve with chewy sourdough bread.

CHICKEN, BROCCOLI, LEMON, AND RICE SOUP

7 cups chicken stock
6 chicken thighs
2 large garlic cloves, lightly smashed with flat side of knife
4 cups coarsely chopped broccoli florets (not thick stems)
2 whole green onions, chopped
½ cup fresh basil leaves, shredded

2 tablespoons fresh lemon juice
Salt
Freshly ground black pepper
2 cups cooked long-grain white or brown rice
¼ cup freshly grated Romano cheese, plus extra for serving

BRING CHICKEN STOCK to a boil in large saucepan. Add chicken, reduce heat, and simmer gently, skimming foam and impurities, for 10 minutes or until stock is clear. Add garlic and continue simmering for 30 minutes or until chicken is cooked through; remove chicken to plate and set aside until cool enough to handle. Skim off any fat from soup.

Tear chicken into shreds, discarding skin and bones. Add chicken, broccoli, green onions, basil, lemon juice, salt, pepper, and rice and cook for 5 minutes or just until heated through and broccoli is just tender. Stir in cheese. Ladle into soup bowls and serve with extra cheese. Serves 4.

EASY CHICKEN AND RICE SOUP

7 cups chicken stock
6 chicken thighs
2 large garlic cloves, lightly
  smashed with flat side
  of knife
2 cups diced carrots
2 medium ribs celery,
  finely chopped
¾ cup fresh flat-leaf
  parsley, chopped

½ teaspoon dried thyme
1 small bay leaf
3 whole green onions,
  chopped
2 cups cooked long-grain
  white or brown rice
Salt
Freshly ground black
  pepper
Lime wedges (optional)

BRING CHICKEN STOCK to a boil in large saucepan. Add chicken, reduce heat, and simmer gently, skimming foam and impurities, for 10 minutes or until stock is clear. Add garlic and continue simmering for 30 minutes or until chicken is cooked through; remove chicken to plate and set aside until cool enough to handle. Skim off any fat from soup.

Add carrots, celery, parsley, thyme, and bay leaf. Cover, and simmer for 20 minutes or until vegetables are tender.

Tear chicken into shreds, discarding skin and bones. Add chicken, green onions, rice, salt, and pepper and cook for 2 minutes or just until heated through. Remove bay leaf and serve with wedges of lime if desired. Serves 4.

At the first sign of a sniffle, I whip up this soothing, quick-and-easy "penicillin." It works every time! It also makes a fine lunch or supper any time. ◆ Chicken thighs have lots of flavor – and are chock-full of nutrients – so please don't substitute chicken breasts.

Known as "congee" or "jook," this thick rice soup is typically eaten for breakfast or at any time of day as a complete meal. ♦ It's difficult to describe the flavor the rice, water, a little chicken stock (don't be tempted to add more), and ginger impart, except to say they cook up into a soothing soup that's brought to life by the addition of a small handful of crunchy, salty peanuts, sharp green onions, and cilantro, and finished with a generous drizzle of sesame oil. ♦ Congee is the perfect antidote for that one-glass-of-wine-too-many syndrome, or when you're simply feeling under the weather. ♦ Search out (in Asian markets) Rose Brand, Extra Super Quality, Pin Kiew Glutinous Rice from Thailand (it has an illustration of a rose on the bag) for the absolute ultimate congee. Be sure to buy whole rice kernels – not broken rice.

CHINESE RICE SOUP

1 cup Thai Rose Brand
   glutinous rice
11 cups water
1 cup chicken stock (if
   canned, undiluted)
2 quarter-size slices
   fresh ginger

2 teaspoons salt
1 tablespoon vegetable oil
Roasted peanuts
Chopped green onions
Chopped fresh cilantro
   leaves
Sesame oil

PLACE RICE in strainer and rinse under cold running water, swirling it with your hands several times until water runs fairly clear. Place drained rice, water, chicken stock, ginger, salt, and vegetable oil in very large saucepan or soup kettle. Bring to a boil, reduce heat, and simmer, stirring occasionally, for 1 hour or until rice turns into a thin, creamy porridge; remove ginger. Serve with separate bowls of peanuts, green onions, and cilantro for each person to add to taste and pass the sesame oil. Serves 8.

WILD RICE AND MUSHROOM SOUP

¼ cup (½ stick) butter
2 large garlic cloves,
    chopped
1 medium onion, chopped
½ teaspoon dried thyme
1 cup wild rice
6 cups chicken stock
½ pound combination of
    fresh shiitake and oyster
    mushrooms, stems
    discarded, coarsely
    chopped

Salt
Freshly ground black
    pepper
½ cup half-and-half

MELT 2 TABLESPOONS butter in large saucepan over medium-high heat. Add garlic, onion, and thyme and cook for 2 minutes or until tender. Add rice and stir to combine. Add chicken stock and bring to a boil. Reduce heat, cover, and simmer for 45 minutes or until rice is tender but still chewy.

Melt remaining butter in medium skillet over medium-high heat. Add mushrooms and cook for 1 minute or just until tender. Stir mushrooms, salt, pepper, and half-and-half into soup and cook until heated through. Serve at once. Serves 6 to 8.

If you love nutty-tasting wild rice and woodsy wild mushrooms as much as I do, then you'll love this soup! It's both elegant and earthy – a perfect prelude to a fall or winter dinner. ◆ Don't make the soup too far in advance, the rice thickens considerably on standing.

Quick as a wink to cook, and nicely nippy with cayenne and Tabasco. ◆ If you're the least bit okra-shy, this soup is sure to change your mind. If you love okra, well, what are you waiting for?! ◆ The soup must be freshly made just before serving, as frozen okra loses its color, texture, and flavor very fast.

TOMATO, OKRA, AND RICE SOUP

1 tablespoon olive oil	½ teaspoon cayenne
1 large garlic clove, chopped	½ teaspoon Tabasco
1 small onion, chopped	1 bay leaf
	Salt
28-ounce can tomatoes, undrained, puréed in food processor	Freshly ground black pepper
2 cups water	¼ cup long-grain white rice
1 teaspoon dried basil	1 pound frozen whole okra, partially thawed, sliced into ½-inch rounds, stem ends discarded
1 teaspoon dried oregano	
½ teaspoon dried thyme	

HEAT OIL in heavy medium saucepan over medium-high heat. Add garlic and onion and cook for 2 minutes or until tender. Add puréed tomatoes, water, basil, oregano, thyme, cayenne, Tabasco, bay leaf, salt, pepper, and rice. Reduce heat, and simmer for 20 minutes or until rice is tender. Add okra and simmer for 5 minutes or just until cooked through and still bright green. Remove bay leaf and serve at once. Serves 6.

THAI LEMON-LIME SHRIMP AND RICE-NOODLE SOUP

2 ounces rice-stick noodles
1 pound raw medium
    shrimp in shells
1 tablespoon vegetable oil
6 cups chicken stock
3 stalks lemon grass, cut
    into 1-inch pieces, or zest
    of 1 lemon
½ teaspoon hot red
    pepper flakes
2 tablespoons fresh
    lime juice

2 tablespoons Thai
    fish sauce
2 rings canned pineapple,
    coarsely diced
½ cup canned straw
    mushrooms, drained,
    thinly sliced
¼ cup shredded coconut,
    toasted
Fresh basil leaves,
    shredded
Fresh cilantro leaves

BREAK NOODLES into 2-inch pieces, add to medium bowl, and cover with hot tap water. Soak for 5 minutes or just until soft. Drain well and set aside.

Peel and devein shrimp, leaving tail on and reserving shells. In large saucepan, heat oil and cook shells until they turn pink. Add chicken stock and lemon grass. Bring to a boil, reduce heat, and simmer for 20 minutes. Strain stock, discarding shells and lemon grass, return to pan, and bring back to a boil. Add red pepper flakes, shrimp, and noodles and cook for 2 minutes or just until cooked through. Stir in lime juice, fish sauce, pineapple, mushrooms, and toasted coconut. Remove from heat. Garnish each serving with basil and cilantro. Serve at once. Serves 4 to 6.

Emphatically seasoned with chiles and citrus, this is my take on Thailand's favorite soup. ◆ *Fresh herbs and Thai fish sauce are essential. They are available in Asian markets and some supermarkets.* ◆ *Rice-stick noodles are also called rice vermicelli.*

saucepan

RISOTTO

◆ ◆ ◆

V

ivid in color, this side-dish risotto is tempting with almost any entrée. ◆ Garnish each serving with julienne strips of beet leaves if desired.

BEET RISOTTO

About 3 cups chicken stock
1 tablespoon olive oil
2 tablespoons butter
1 large garlic clove, chopped
1 small onion, chopped
¾ cup finely diced peeled raw beets (not canned)
1 cup Arborio rice
½ cup French dry white vermouth or chicken stock
Grated zest of 1 large lemon
¼ cup freshly grated Parmesan cheese, plus extra for serving
Salt

BRING CHICKEN STOCK to a simmer in small saucepan over high heat. Reduce heat to low.

Heat oil and 1 tablespoon butter in heavy medium saucepan over medium-high heat. Add garlic, onion, and beets and cook for 2 minutes or until onion is tender. Add rice and stir to coat with oil. Add vermouth, stirring constantly, until most of the liquid is absorbed, about 1 minute. Reduce heat to medium and add ½ cup hot chicken stock and stir until most is absorbed. Repeat this process for about 20 minutes, adding stock ½ cup at a time, stirring frequently, and tasting toward end of cooking until rice is creamy but al dente (tender, yet slightly firm). (Not all the stock may be needed.)

Stir in lemon zest, cheese, salt, and remaining butter and remove pan from heat. Serve at once. Pass extra cheese. Serves 4.

RISOTTO WITH LEMON

About 3 cups chicken stock
1 tablespoon olive oil
1 large garlic clove,
    chopped
1 small onion, chopped
1 cup Arborio rice
½ cup French dry white
    vermouth or chicken
    stock

2 tablespoons butter
Grated zest of 1 medium
    lemon
2 tablespoons fresh
    lemon juice
¼ cup freshly grated
    Parmesan cheese, plus
    extra for serving

BRING CHICKEN STOCK to a simmer in small saucepan over high heat. Reduce heat to low.

Heat oil in heavy medium saucepan over medium-high heat. Add garlic and onion and cook for 2 minutes or until tender. Add rice and stir to coat with oil. Add vermouth, stirring constantly, until most of the liquid is absorbed, about 1 minute. Reduce heat to medium and add ½ cup hot chicken stock and stir until most is absorbed. Repeat this process for about 20 minutes, adding stock ½ cup at a time, stirring frequently, and tasting toward end of cooking until rice is creamy but al dente (tender, yet slightly firm). (Not all the stock may be needed.)

Stir in butter, lemon zest, lemon juice, and cheese and remove pan from heat. Serve at once. Pass the peppermill and extra cheese. Serves 4.

Zesty with lemon and buttery smooth, this makes a wonderful entrée, first course, or an accompaniment to grilled chicken or seafood. ◆ *I like the pure lemon flavor, but feel free to add some chopped fresh herbs such as mint, chives, dill, parsley or sage with the lemon zest if you wish.*

Yellow with saffron, this is the classic Risotto alla Milanese, from the Italian city of the same name. Traditionally served with Osso Buco (braised veal shanks), it also goes well with roasted or grilled poultry.

SAFFRON RISOTTO

About 3 cups chicken stock
1 tablespoon olive oil
1 small onion, chopped
1 cup Arborio rice
¼ teaspoon saffron threads
  (not powdered)
½ cup French dry white
  vermouth or chicken
  stock

2 tablespoons butter
¼ cup freshly grated
  Parmesan cheese, plus
  extra for serving
Salt
Freshly ground black
  pepper

BRING CHICKEN STOCK to a simmer in small saucepan over high heat. Reduce heat to low.

Heat oil in heavy medium saucepan over medium-high heat. Add onion and cook for 2 minutes or until tender. Add rice and saffron and stir to coat with oil. Add vermouth, stirring constantly, until most of the liquid is absorbed, about 1 minute. Reduce heat to medium and add ½ cup hot chicken stock and stir until most is absorbed. Repeat this process for about 20 minutes, adding stock ½ cup at a time, stirring frequently, and tasting toward end of cooking until rice is creamy but al dente (tender, yet slightly firm). (Not all the stock may be needed.)

Stir in butter, cheese, salt, and pepper and remove pan from heat. Serve at once. Pass extra cheese. Serves 4.

PUMPKIN RISOTTO

About 3 cups chicken stock
1 tablespoon olive oil
1 large garlic clove, chopped
1 small onion, chopped
¼ teaspoon hot red pepper flakes (optional)
1 cup Arborio rice
½ cup French dry white vermouth or chicken stock

1 cup cooked fresh pumpkin (not canned)
1 tablespoon butter
Salt
Freshly ground black pepper
½ cup freshly grated Parmesan cheese
Grated zest of 1 large lemon
Parmesan cheese, shaved

BRING CHICKEN STOCK to a simmer in small saucepan over high heat. Reduce heat to low.

Heat oil in heavy medium saucepan over medium-high heat. Add garlic, onion, and red pepper flakes and cook for 2 minutes or until tender. Add rice and stir to coat with oil. Add vermouth, stirring constantly, until most of the liquid is absorbed, about 1 minute, then add pumpkin. Reduce heat to medium and add ½ cup hot chicken stock and stir until most is absorbed. Repeat this process for about 20 minutes, adding stock ½ cup at a time, stirring frequently, and tasting toward end of cooking until rice is creamy but al dente (tender, yet slightly firm). (Not all the stock may be needed.)

Stir in butter, salt, pepper, cheese, and lemon zest and remove pan from heat. Garnish each serving with shavings of Parmesan cheese and serve at once. Serves 4.

P*umpkin adds sweetness and a pale orange hue to this risotto which is a perfect complement to roast turkey, duck, chicken, or veal.* ◆ *You may substitute butternut squash for the pumpkin.*

This rich and cheesy risotto is cousin to the classic four-cheese pasta sauce. ◆ Try these variations: substitute 2 ounces Fontina cheese for the Cambozola; or 4 ounces Mascarpone cheese and 2 tablespoons Parmesan; or use 4 ounces Camembert or Brie; or experiment with different combinations of your favorite cheeses.

RISOTTO WITH FOUR CHEESES

About 3 cups chicken stock
1 tablespoon olive oil
1 large garlic clove, chopped
1 small onion, chopped
1 cup Arborio rice
½ cup French dry white vermouth or chicken stock
2 ounces Cambozola or Gorgonzola cheese, crumbled, at room temperature
2 ounces Fontina cheese, diced, at room temperature
1 tablespoon freshly grated Parmesan cheese
1 tablespoon freshly grated Romano cheese
Freshly ground black pepper

BRING CHICKEN STOCK to a simmer in small saucepan over high heat. Reduce heat to low.

Heat oil in heavy medium saucepan over medium-high heat. Add garlic and onion and cook for 2 minutes or until tender. Add rice and stir to coat with oil. Add vermouth, stirring constantly, until most of the liquid is absorbed, about 1 minute. Reduce heat to medium and add ½ cup hot chicken stock and stir until most is absorbed. Repeat this process for about 20 minutes, adding stock ½ cup at a time, stirring frequently, and tasting toward end of cooking until rice is creamy but al dente (tender, yet slightly firm). (Not all the stock may be needed.)

Stir in the four cheeses and pepper and remove pan from heat. Serve at once. Pass the peppermill. Serves 4.

RISOTTO WITH GORGONZOLA AND PISTACHIOS

About 3 cups chicken stock
1 tablespoon olive oil
1 large garlic clove, chopped
1 small onion, chopped
1 cup Arborio rice
½ cup French dry white vermouth or chicken stock
½ cup crumbled Gorgonzola cheese

¼ cup freshly grated Parmesan cheese, plus extra for serving
Freshly ground black pepper
¼ cup chopped natural-colored shelled pistachios

BRING CHICKEN STOCK to a simmer in small saucepan over high heat. Reduce heat to low.

Heat oil in heavy medium saucepan over medium-high heat. Add garlic and onion and cook for 2 minutes or until tender. Add rice and stir to coat with oil. Add vermouth, stirring constantly, until most of the liquid is absorbed, about 1 minute. Reduce heat to medium and add ½ cup hot chicken stock and stir until most is absorbed. Repeat this process for about 20 minutes, adding stock ½ cup at a time, stirring frequently, and tasting toward end of cooking until rice is creamy but al dente (tender, yet slightly firm). (Not all the stock may be needed.)

Stir in Gorgonzola, Parmesan, pepper, and 2 tablespoons chopped pistachios and remove pan from heat. Spoon onto warmed plates, garnish with remaining nuts, and serve at once. Pass the peppermill and extra Parmesan. Serves 4.

Luscious with creamy Gorgonzola, this risotto deserves a robust red wine and a salad of mixed baby lettuces dressed with a lemon vinaigrette. If pistachios are unavailable, lightly toasted pecans may be used. ◆ By the way, this is also delicious made with Torta di Gorgonzola instead of Gorgonzola.

D elicately tangy young chèvre (goat cheese), sweet sun-dried tomatoes, and fresh green basil strike a thoroughly modern note and lend a rich, sensuous flavor to risotto. ◆ Risotto must be served the instant it is ready – it can't be made ahead and reheated – like time and pasta, it waits for no one!

RISOTTO WITH CHÈVRE AND SUN-DRIED TOMATOES

About 3 cups chicken stock
1 tablespoon olive oil
1 large garlic clove, chopped
1 small onion, chopped
¼ teaspoon hot red pepper flakes
1 cup Arborio rice
½ cup French dry white vermouth or chicken stock

10 large sun-dried tomato halves in oil, drained, diced
4 ounces soft, mild chèvre, crumbled
2 tablespoons freshly grated Parmesan cheese
1 tablespoon chopped fresh basil leaves, plus extra for garnish

BRING CHICKEN STOCK to a simmer in small saucepan over high heat. Reduce heat to low.

Heat oil in heavy medium saucepan over medium-high heat. Add garlic, onion, and red pepper flakes and cook for 2 minutes or until tender. Add rice and stir to coat with oil. Add vermouth, stirring constantly, until most of the liquid is absorbed, about 1 minute. Reduce heat to medium and add ½ cup hot chicken stock and stir until most is absorbed. Repeat this process for about 20 minutes, adding stock ½ cup at a time, stirring frequently, and tasting toward end of cooking until rice is creamy but al dente (tender, yet slightly firm). (Not all the stock may be needed.)

Stir in sun-dried tomatoes, chèvre, Parmesan, and basil and remove pan from heat. Garnish each serving with basil and serve at once. Serves 4.

RISOTTO WITH CHILES AND MONTEREY JACK CHEESE

About 3 cups chicken stock
1 tablespoon olive oil
1 large garlic clove, chopped
1 small onion, chopped
1 cup Arborio rice
¼ cup French dry white vermouth or chicken stock
¼ cup pickled sliced jalapeños, drained, coarsely chopped
1 cup grated Monterey Jack cheese
¼ cup freshly grated Parmesan cheese
Chopped fresh cilantro for garnish

BRING CHICKEN STOCK to a simmer in small saucepan over high heat. Reduce heat to low.

Heat oil in heavy medium saucepan over medium-high heat. Add garlic and onion and cook for 2 minutes or until tender. Add rice and stir to coat with oil. Add vermouth, stirring constantly, until most of the liquid is absorbed, about 1 minute. Reduce heat to medium and add ½ cup hot chicken stock and stir until most is absorbed. Repeat this process for about 20 minutes, adding stock ½ cup at a time, stirring frequently, and tasting toward end of cooking until rice is creamy but al dente (tender, yet slightly firm). (Not all the stock may be needed.)

Stir in chiles, Monterey Jack and Parmesan cheeses and remove from heat. Garnish with cilantro and serve at once. Serves 4.

Tex-Mex ingredients — jalapeños, cilantro, and Monterey Jack — flavor this unorthodox and uncommonly tasty risotto. ♦ *The texture is extra-creamy and it's fairly hot — so add more chiles only if you dare!*

cilantro

RISOTTO WITH SHRIMP

Feel free to use a mixture of seafood – shrimp, scallops, calamari, or steamed mussels – in this elegant risotto. Or – for a luscious lobster risotto – substitute 1 pound cooked lobster meat.

About 3 cups fish or chicken stock
2 tablespoons olive oil
1 pound raw medium shrimp, peeled, deveined, patted dry
1 large garlic clove, chopped
1 small onion, chopped
½ teaspoon dried basil
1 cup Arborio rice

½ cup French dry white vermouth or stock
¼ teaspoon saffron threads (not powdered)
¼ cup freshly grated Parmesan cheese, plus extra for serving
Freshly ground black pepper
Shredded fresh basil for garnish

BRING FISH or chicken stock to a simmer in small saucepan over high heat. Reduce heat to low.

Heat 1 tablespoon oil in medium nonstick skillet over medium-high heat. Add shrimp and cook for 2 minutes or just until opaque. Transfer to plate; set aside.

Add remaining oil to pan, heat, and add garlic, onion, and dried basil and cook for 2 minutes or until tender. Add rice and stir to coat with oil. Add vermouth, stirring constantly, until most of the liquid is absorbed, about 1 minute, then add saffron. Reduce heat to medium, add ½ cup hot stock, and stir until most is absorbed. Repeat this process for about 20 minutes, adding stock ½ cup at a time, stirring frequently, and tasting toward end of cooking until rice is creamy but al dente (tender, yet slightly firm). (Not all the stock may be needed.)

Stir in cheese, pepper, and shrimp, cook for 2 minutes or just until heated through, and remove pan from heat. Garnish with basil and serve at once. Pass extra cheese. Serves 4.

RISOTTO WITH SMOKED SALMON AND DILL

About 3 cups chicken stock
1 tablespoon olive oil
1 large garlic clove, chopped
1 small onion, chopped
1 cup Arborio rice
½ cup French dry white vermouth or chicken stock
½ pound thinly sliced smoked salmon, coarsely chopped

¼ cup fresh dill, chopped
¼ cup freshly grated Parmesan cheese, plus extra for serving
Freshly ground black pepper
Tiny capers for garnish
Grated zest of 1 medium lemon for garnish

BRING CHICKEN STOCK to a simmer in small saucepan over high heat. Reduce heat to low.

Heat oil in heavy medium saucepan over medium-high heat. Add garlic and onion and cook for 2 minutes or until tender. Add rice and stir to coat with oil. Add vermouth, stirring constantly, until most of the liquid is absorbed, about 1 minute. Reduce heat to medium and add ½ cup hot chicken stock and stir until most is absorbed. Repeat this process for about 20 minutes, adding stock ½ cup at a time, stirring frequently, and tasting toward end of cooking until rice is creamy but al dente (tender, yet slightly firm). (Not all the stock may be needed.)

Stir in smoked salmon, dill, cheese, and pepper and remove pan from heat. Garnish each serving with a generous sprinkling of capers and lemon zest. Serve at once. Pass extra cheese. Serves 4.

Beautiful pink smoked salmon is a strikingly attractive addition to risotto. ◆ I came up with the idea recently when I happened upon a little leftover smoked salmon. It makes a perfectly gorgeous first course or entrée (especially if you just happen upon a little Champagne!).

E

*xotic or "wild" mushrooms –
shiitake, porcini, or oyster –
bring an earthy, yet eloquent
tone to risotto.* ◆ *Fabulous as
a luncheon or light dinner entrée teamed
with a tart green salad.*

RISOTTO WITH WILD MUSHROOMS

About 3 cups chicken stock
1 tablespoon olive oil
3 tablespoons butter
1 large garlic clove, chopped
1 small onion, chopped
½ pound fresh wild mushrooms (combination of shiitake, porcini, or oyster), stems discarded, sliced
1 cup Arborio rice
½ cup French dry white vermouth or chicken stock
¼ cup freshly grated Parmesan cheese
Salt
Freshly ground black pepper
¼ cup fresh flat-leaf parsley, chopped

BRING CHICKEN STOCK to a simmer in small saucepan over high heat. Reduce heat to low.

Heat oil and 1 tablespoon butter in heavy medium saucepan over medium-high heat. Add garlic, onion, and mushrooms and cook for 2 minutes or just until mushrooms begin to brown. Add rice and stir to coat with oil. Add vermouth, stirring constantly, until most of the liquid is absorbed, about 1 minute. Reduce heat to medium and add ½ cup hot chicken stock and stir until most is absorbed. Repeat this process for about 20 minutes, adding stock ½ cup at a time, stirring frequently, and tasting toward end of cooking until rice is creamy but al dente (tender, yet slightly firm). (Not all the stock may be needed.)

Stir in remaining butter, cheese, salt, pepper, and parsley and remove pan from heat. Serve at once. Pass the peppermill. Serves 4.

RISOTTO WITH MARINATED ARTICHOKES AND ROASTED RED PEPPERS

About 3 cups chicken stock
1 tablespoon olive oil
1 large garlic clove, chopped
¼ cup chopped onion
2 ounces thinly sliced prosciutto, chopped
1 cup Arborio rice
½ cup French dry white vermouth or chicken stock
1 tablespoon butter
¼ cup freshly grated Parmesan cheese, plus extra for serving
6-ounce jar marinated artichoke hearts, drained, coarsely chopped
½ cup homemade or bottled roasted red peppers, drained, coarsely chopped
Chopped fresh flat-leaf parsley for garnish

BRING CHICKEN STOCK to a simmer in small saucepan over high heat. Reduce heat to low.

Heat oil in heavy medium saucepan over medium-high heat. Add garlic, onion, and prosciutto and cook for 2 minutes or until tender. Add rice and stir to coat with oil. Add vermouth, stirring constantly, until most of the liquid is absorbed, about 1 minute. Reduce heat to medium and add ½ cup hot chicken stock and stir until most is absorbed. Repeat this process for about 20 minutes, adding stock ½ cup at a time, stirring frequently, and tasting toward end of cooking until rice is creamy but al dente (tender, yet slightly firm). (Not all the stock may be needed.)

Stir in butter, Parmesan, artichokes, and red peppers and remove pan from heat. Garnish with parsley and serve at once. Pass the peppermill and extra cheese. Serves 4.

P*retty and colorful, here I've embellished risotto with pale green artichokes, bright red roasted peppers, and bites of prosciutto for an absolutely irresistible result. ◆ Serve with a crisp green salad and a chilled Italian white wine, followed by fruit and cheese and perhaps a cup of espresso or cappuccino, and wait for the compliments!*

R isotto variations are endless and endlessly pleasing. Here, sweet Italian sausage and tomato combine to create a really wonderful, full-flavored dish. ◆ Just add a bottle of red wine and a crunchy salad and imagine yourself (back) in Northern Italy. Buon appetito!

RISOTTO WITH SWEET ITALIAN SAUSAGE AND TOMATO

About 3 cups chicken stock
1 tablespoon olive oil
½ pound sweet Italian sausage, casings removed, crumbled
1 large garlic clove, chopped
1 small onion, chopped
¼ teaspoon dried basil
⅛ teaspoon hot red pepper flakes
1 cup Arborio rice
½ cup French dry white vermouth or chicken stock
1 large ripe tomato, seeded, coarsely chopped
¼ cup freshly grated Parmesan cheese, plus extra for serving
1 tablespoon chopped fresh basil leaves

BRING CHICKEN STOCK to a simmer in small saucepan over high heat. Reduce heat to low.

Heat oil in heavy medium saucepan over medium-high heat. Add sausage and cook until no pink remains. Transfer meat to plate; discard all but 1 tablespoon oil. Add garlic, onion, dried basil, and red pepper flakes and cook for 2 minutes or until tender. Add rice and stir to coat with oil. Add vermouth, stirring constantly until most of the liquid is absorbed, about 1 minute. Reduce heat to medium and add ½ cup hot chicken stock and stir until most is absorbed. Repeat this process for about 20 minutes, adding stock ½ cup at a time, stirring frequently, and tasting toward end of cooking until rice is creamy but al dente (tender, yet slightly firm). (Not all the stock may be needed.)

Add sausage and tomato and cook for 2 minutes or just until heated through. Stir in cheese and fresh basil and remove pan from heat. Serve at once. Pass the peppermill and extra cheese. Serves 4.

ENTRÉES

♦ ♦ ♦

Traditionally, Spain's national dish is cooked in a large shallow pan called a paetella – I use a large skillet – and short-grain Valencia rice is more authentic than the scented rice I've chosen here. ◆ Paella typically contains shrimp, squid, clams, mussels, chicken, and sausage, but I've simplified the recipe somewhat by using fewer ingredients. ◆ Serve with an icy, red-wine Sangria and a refreshing salad of sliced oranges, red onion, and Kalamata olives drizzled with a lemon-garlic vinaigrette, and you can almost hear the castanets. Olé!

Easy Paella

1 tablespoon olive oil
2 skinless, boneless chicken breast halves, cut into ½-inch thick strips
½ pound chorizo, sweet Italian, or garlic sausage, cut into ¼-inch thick slices
4 large garlic cloves, chopped
1 medium-small onion, chopped
¼ teaspoon hot red pepper flakes
1½ cups Jasmine rice, rinsed

2½ cups chicken stock (more if needed)
½ teaspoon saffron threads (not powdered)
½ pound cooked small (salad) shrimp
½ cup homemade or bottled roasted red peppers, drained, cut into strips
½ cup fresh or frozen tiny peas
¼ cup fresh flat-leaf parsley, chopped
Grated zest of 1 medium lemon

HEAT OIL in large nonstick skillet over medium-high heat. Add chicken and cook for 4 minutes or just until lightly browned and cooked through; remove to plate. Add sausage and cook for 5 minutes or until cooked through; remove to plate. Add garlic, onion, and red pepper flakes and cook for 2 minutes. Add rice and stir to coat with oil. Add chicken stock and saffron and bring to a boil. Cover, reduce heat, and cook for 15 minutes or until liquid is absorbed and rice is tender, stirring occasionally. (If necessary add about ¼ cup stock if rice is too firm and continue cooking, covered.) Stir in chicken, sausage, shrimp, roasted red peppers, peas, parsley, and lemon zest. Cook, stirring, for 5 minutes, uncovered, or until heated through. Serves 4 to 6.

SHRIMP JAMBALAYA

2 tablespoons olive oil
1 pound raw medium
  shrimp, peeled,
  deveined, patted dry
4 large garlic cloves,
  chopped
1 medium-small onion,
  chopped
1 cup long-grain white rice
½ teaspoon dried basil
½ teaspoon dried thyme
½ teaspoon cayenne

½ teaspoon salt
½ cup homemade or
  bottled roasted red
  peppers, drained,
  coarsely chopped
1¾ cups chicken stock
½ teaspoon Tabasco
1 large green onion (green
  part only), chopped
¼ cup fresh flat-leaf parsley,
  chopped

HEAT 1 TABLESPOON oil in large heavy saucepan over medium-high heat. Add shrimp and cook for 2 minutes or just until opaque; remove to plate.

Add remaining oil to pan, heat, and add garlic and onion and cook for 2 minutes or until tender. Add rice, basil, thyme, cayenne, salt, and roasted peppers; stir to combine. Add chicken stock and Tabasco and bring to a boil. Cover, reduce heat to medium-low, and cook for 15 minutes or until liquid is absorbed and rice is tender. Stir in shrimp, cover, and cook for 4 minutes or until heated through. Stir in green onion and parsley. Remove from heat and let stand, uncovered, for 5 minutes before serving. Serves 2 to 4.

J azzy Jambalaya – originally invented as a way to use up leftovers – usually contains a combination of seafood, smoked meats, and chicken. ♦ My version is lighter than most. It's pretty with pink shrimp and roasted red peppers and is mildly hot. Add more Tabasco or offer it at the table for those who wish to turn up the heat.

E touffée means "smothered" in French. In Creole cooking this translates into smothered in its own juices with plenty of butter and spice. ♦ The colors are dazzling, the eating downright delicious.

SHRIMP ÉTOUFFÉE

1 tablespoon olive oil
4 large garlic cloves, chopped
1 teaspoon cayenne
1½ pounds raw medium shrimp, peeled, deveined, patted dry
About 4 tablespoons butter
4 whole green onions, chopped
1 medium-small sweet red pepper, seeded, diced
1 medium-small sweet yellow pepper, seeded, diced
¾ pound ripe cherry tomatoes, quartered
Salt
Freshly ground black pepper
¾ cup fish or chicken stock
Hot cooked long-grain white rice (page 63)

HEAT OIL in large nonstick skillet over medium-high heat. Add garlic, ½ teaspoon cayenne, and shrimp and cook for 2 minutes or just until opaque; remove to plate.

Add 1 tablespoon butter to pan, add green onions, red and yellow peppers, and cook for 1 minute or just until tender-crisp. Add tomatoes, salt, pepper, and remaining cayenne; cook another 1 minute or just until tomatoes are heated through. Reduce heat, add stock, and simmer for a few minutes or until slightly reduced. Add remaining butter 1 tablespoon at a time, stirring in one direction, until slightly thickened. Add more butter – a tablespoon at a time – if you prefer a richer, creamier sauce. Add shrimp and allow to just heat through – don't overcook. Serve at once with hot cooked rice. Serves 4.

'50s STYLE SHRIMP CURRY

4 tablespoons butter
2 tablespoons all-purpose
  flour
2 tablespoons best-quality
  curry powder
1 large garlic clove, finely
  chopped
1 small onion, chopped
½ sweet red pepper,
  seeded, diced
2 ripe medium tomatoes,
  chopped
1 bay leaf
Salt
Freshly ground black
  pepper

Grated zest of 1 large lemon
1 tablespoon fresh
  lemon juice
1⅓ cups chicken stock
1 pound raw medium
  shrimp, peeled, deveined
3 tablespoons French dry
  white vermouth
Hot cooked long-grain
  white rice (page 63)
Chopped apple
Raisins
Shredded sweet coconut
Sliced bananas

MELT BUTTER in large nonstick skillet over medium heat. Stir in flour and curry powder. Add garlic, onion, red pepper, tomatoes, bay leaf, salt, pepper, lemon zest, and lemon juice and cook for 2 minutes or until onion is tender. Add chicken stock and simmer, stirring, for 10 minutes. Add shrimp and vermouth and cook for 2 minutes or just until shrimp are cooked through. Discard bay leaf. Serve with rice and separate bowls of apple, raisins, coconut, and bananas for each person to add to taste. Serves 2 to 4.

Just before Drew and I were married, my mother passed along a recipe of hers that she devised in the '50s. This dish used to be one of our favorites, and when I came upon it while searching through my files, I thought it would be fun to cook it again 25 years later! It has lost none of its appeal – it's still delectable and absolutely sensational. ◆ My modernized version uses lemon zest and a sweet red – not green – pepper.

Utterly delectable. ◆ Sweet shrimp teamed with rice, tomatoes, herbs, lemon zest, and a jolt of salty feta is an effortless dish that never fails to win rave reviews.

SHRIMP AND RICE WITH FETA CHEESE

1 cup long-grain white rice
1¾ cups water
½ teaspoon salt
1 tablespoon olive oil
2 large garlic cloves, chopped
2 whole green onions, chopped (green part separated)
¼ teaspoon cayenne
½ teaspoon dried oregano
½ teaspoon dried basil
1 pound raw medium shrimp, peeled, deveined, patted dry
¾ pound cherry tomatoes, quartered
½ cup fresh flat-leaf parsley, chopped
Grated zest of 1 medium lemon
⅓ cup crumbled feta cheese

BRING RICE, water, and salt to a boil in heavy medium saucepan over high heat. Cover, reduce heat to medium-low, and cook for 15 minutes or until liquid is absorbed and rice is tender; keep covered on low heat.

When rice is ready, heat oil in large nonstick skillet over medium-high heat. Add garlic, white part of green onions, cayenne, oregano, basil, and shrimp and cook for 2 minutes or just until shrimp are opaque. Add tomatoes and cook for 1 minute or just until heated through. Sprinkle with parsley and lemon zest. Add rice and stir until combined. Sprinkle with remaining green onions and feta cheese. Serves 2 to 4.

BAYOU DIRTY RICE

2 slices bacon, diced
½ pound ground pork
½ pound chicken livers,
  trimmed, patted dry,
  finely chopped
2 large garlic cloves,
  chopped
1 small onion, chopped
1 medium sweet green
  pepper, seeded, diced
½ cup homemade or
  bottled roasted red
  peppers, drained,
  chopped

½ teaspoon cayenne
Freshly ground black
  pepper
½ teaspoon salt
½ teaspoon dried thyme
1¾ cups chicken stock
½ teaspoon Tabasco
1 cup long-grain white rice
1 large green onion (green
  part only), chopped
¾ cup fresh parsley,
  chopped

COOK BACON until beginning to crisp in heavy medium saucepan over medium-high heat. Add pork and cook, breaking up meat with fork until no pink remains. Add chicken livers and cook for 1 minute or until cooked through; remove meat mixture to plate and set aside.

Add garlic, onion, and green pepper and cook for 2 minutes or until tender. Stir in roasted red peppers, cayenne, pepper, salt, and thyme. Add chicken stock, Tabasco, and rice and bring to a boil. Cover, reduce heat to medium-low, and cook for 15 minutes or until liquid is absorbed and rice is tender. Add meat mixture, stir to combine thoroughly, cover, and cook for 5 minutes. Stir in green onion and parsley. Serves 4 to 6.

C hicken livers impart a dark coloring, hence the name "dirty" rice. ◆ Cajuns enjoy this hearty, homey rice concoction as a cheap-and-cheerful one-dish meal, or as a side dish to fried chicken or pork barbecue. ◆ I've taken the liberty of brightening the dish with some roasted red peppers.

Sweet and sour crisp-fried Thai noodles are a spectacular dish that is well worth the effort. ◆ Don't be daunted by the number of ingredients and steps: the noodles can be prepared several hours ahead and set aside, uncovered, then warmed in a 200°F oven just before serving. The omelet can be done ahead, covered, and refrigerated. The sauce can be mixed ahead, too. Then everything is cooked up in merely minutes.

THAI MEE KROB

4 ounces rice-stick noodles
3 cups vegetable oil
1 large egg, beaten
¼ cup ketchup
1 tablespoon sugar
2 tablespoons Thai fish sauce
1 tablespoon fresh lime juice
1 large garlic clove, chopped
½ pound ground pork

1 pound raw medium shrimp, peeled, deveined, patted dry
Grated zest of 1 large orange
2 whole green onions, shredded
¼ pound fresh (not canned) bean sprouts
Fresh cilantro leaves, for garnish

SEPARATE AND break noodles into pieces about 3- to 4-inches long (best done in sink as they tend to fly around).

Heat oil to 360°F in flat-bottomed wok or heavy large deep skillet. Deep-fry noodles in small batches, for a few seconds each, or just until puffed and pure white. Don't allow them to brown. Remove with slotted spoon to drain on paper towels; set aside.

Heat 1 teaspoon oil in nonstick medium skillet over medium-high heat. Pour in egg and make a very thin omelet. Transfer to cutting surface and cut into fine strips; set aside.

Combine ketchup, sugar, fish sauce, and lime juice in bowl; set aside.

Just before serving, preheat oven to 200°F. Place fried noodles on platter and warm in oven; watch carefully so they don't brown.

Heat 1 tablespoon oil in medium skillet over high heat. Add garlic and pork and cook, breaking up meat with fork until no pink remains; remove to plate. Add shrimp and cook for 1 minute or until opaque. Return meat, add ketchup mixture and cook, stirring, until sauce is heated through and slightly thickened. In large bowl, using 2 forks, carefully combine shrimp mixture and noodles so as not to break noodles. Mix in egg strips, orange zest, ⅓ of the green onions, and ½ the bean sprouts. Mound noodles on warmed platter and garnish with remaining green onions, bean sprouts, and cilantro. Serves 2 to 4.

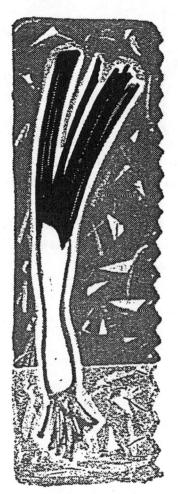

green onion

Simply prepared, a traditional Indian-style pilau uses rice and plenty of spice – curry, cinnamon, and ginger – in this instance. ♦ Basmati or regular long-grain rice are equally good, but be sure to use imported Indian curry powder. ♦ For a real treat, sprinkle with shredded coconut, raisins, and nuts.

QUICK CHICKEN PILAU

1 tablespoon vegetable oil
1 tablespoon butter
2 skinless, boneless chicken breast halves, cut into ¼-inch strips
1 tablespoon finely chopped fresh ginger
1 large garlic clove, chopped
1 medium-small onion, chopped
About 1 tablespoon best-quality curry powder

1-inch piece cinnamon stick
¼ teaspoon hot red pepper flakes
1 cup Basmati rice, rinsed
½ teaspoon salt
About 2 cups chicken stock
½ teaspoon salt
1 cup fresh or frozen tiny peas
Raisins
Shredded coconut
Roasted, unsalted cashews, chopped

HEAT OIL and butter in large nonstick skillet over medium-high heat. Add chicken and cook for 3 minutes or until golden brown. Add ginger, garlic, onion, curry powder to taste, cinnamon stick, and red pepper flakes and cook for 2 minutes or until tender, adding a little more oil or butter if mixture is dry. Add rice and stir to coat with mixture. Add 2 cups chicken stock and salt and bring to a boil. Cover, reduce heat to medium-low, and cook for 15 minutes or until liquid is absorbed and rice is tender. (If rice is too firm, add a little more chicken stock or water, cover, and continue cooking.) Add peas, stir to combine, and cook for 1 minute or until heated through. Serve with separate bowls of raisins, coconut, and cashews for each person to add to taste. Serves 2 to 4.

THAI GREEN CHICKEN CURRY

2 tablespoons vegetable oil
1 large garlic clove, chopped
¼ cup chopped red onion
Grated zest of 1 medium-large lime
1 tablespoon Thai green curry paste
1 tablespoon best-quality curry powder
1½ pounds skinless boneless chicken breasts, cut into ½-inch thick strips

14-ounce can Thai coconut milk
1 tablespoon Thai fish sauce
1 teaspoon brown sugar
½ cup pea-size Thai eggplants or frozen peas, thawed
½ cup fresh basil leaves, shredded
Hot cooked long-grain white or Jasmine rice (page 63)

HEAT OIL in large nonstick skillet over high heat. When hot, add garlic, onion, lime zest, curry paste, and curry powder. Cook, stirring, for 1 minute or until aromatic. Add chicken and stir-fry for 3 minutes or until opaque. Stir in coconut milk, fish sauce, and brown sugar. Reduce heat, add eggplants (if using) and simmer for 7 minutes or until chicken is tender and cooked through. Just before serving, sprinkle with basil and peas (if using), and allow them to just heat through. Serve with hot cooked rice. Serves 2.

Everyone seems to love Thai food these days – and so do I! This chicken-and-rice dish is fiery-hot and fabulous. ♦ Thai green curry paste is usually available in Asian markets, but if not, use the more readily available Thai red curry paste.

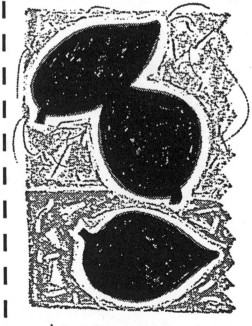

basil

L

ike great stews – cabbage rolls taste even better when made ahead and reheated. ◆ I prefer Savoy cabbage over the more commonplace green variety: its leaves have a more attractive, textured appearance, they are easier to remove, and they take only seconds to cook until pliable.

OLD-FASHIONED CABBAGE ROLLS

8 large Savoy cabbage leaves, cores removed, discarded
4 strips bacon, diced
4 large garlic cloves, chopped
1 large onion, chopped
1 medium sweet red pepper, seeded, diced
1 pound ground pork
1 large egg
½ cup long-grain white rice

1 teaspoon dried thyme
½ teaspoon ground allspice
Salt
Freshly ground black pepper
28-ounce can tomatoes, undrained, puréed in food processor
½ cup French dry white vermouth or chicken stock

BRING A LARGE POT of water to a boil over high heat. Add cabbage leaves and cook for 1 minute or until leaves are pliable. Drain well and set aside.

Cook bacon in medium nonstick skillet over medium-high heat until crisp; discard all but 1 tablespoon fat. Add garlic, onion, and red pepper; cook for 2 minutes or until tender.

Combine half the bacon mixture with pork, egg, rice, thyme, allspice, salt, and pepper in large bowl.

Lay each cabbage leaf flat and divide the mixture evenly among the leaves. Fold in sides of each leaf, then roll up tightly to cover filling. Arrange rolls seam side down in 13- x 8½-inch baking dish. Sprinkle with remaining bacon mixture, pour puréed tomatoes and vermouth over rolls, and cover with aluminum foil. Bake in preheated 400°F oven for 1 hour or until cooked through; remove foil and cook another 20 minutes. Serves 6 to 8.

STUFFED SWEET RED AND YELLOW PEPPERS

1 cup long-grain white rice
1¾ cups water
2 medium-large sweet red peppers, halved lengthwise, seeded
2 medium-large sweet yellow peppers, halved lengthwise, seeded
½ pound ground beef or pork
½ teaspoon salt
Freshly ground black pepper
1 large garlic clove, chopped
2 tablespoons bottled hot pepper rings, drained, chopped
2 whole green onions, chopped
3 medium-large ripe plum tomatoes, seeded, diced
1 teaspoon dried oregano
1 teaspoon dried basil
1 large egg
½ cup freshly grated Parmesan cheese
About 1½ cups coarsely grated mozzarella

My updated version of the ever-popular stuffed green peppers features gorgeous, colorful red and yellow peppers stuffed with a zesty rice mixture. ♦ Another variation to try: use sweet Italian sausage in place of beef or pork; but you may have to reduce the amount of herbs, depending on the sausage seasoning.

BRING RICE and water to a boil in heavy medium saucepan over high heat. Cover, reduce heat to medium-low, and cook for 15 minutes or until water is absorbed and rice is tender. Transfer to large bowl and allow to cool.

Drop peppers into large pot of boiling water and boil for 3 minutes. Drain well and arrange in baking dish just large enough to hold them.

Add meat, salt, pepper, garlic, hot pepper rings, green onions, tomatoes, oregano, basil, egg, and Parmesan cheese to bowl of rice and combine thoroughly.

Preheat oven to 375°F.

Spoon rice mixture into peppers, mounding it slightly, and sprinkle mozzarella on top. Bake for 20 minutes or until stuffing is hot. Serves 6

SPICY SHRIMP GUMBO

G umbos are glorious thick Cajun soup-stews that mingle seafood, chicken or meat with okra, herbs, and spices – all thickened with a roux – oil and flour cooked until browned. ◆ I've simplified the process and practically eliminated the fat (some recipes call for up to 1 cup of oil!). The combo of sweet shrimp and smoky sausage is one of my favorites. ◆ If made ahead, don't add the okra until just before serving. ◆ Smoked kielbasa sausage may be substituted for the andouille.

¼ cup all-purpose flour
1 tablespoon olive oil
½ pound smoked andouille sausage, halved lengthwise, thinly sliced
1 pound raw medium shrimp, peeled, deveined, patted dry
4 large garlic cloves, chopped
4 whole green onions, chopped (green part separated)
½ cup homemade or bottled roasted red peppers, drained, coarsely chopped

Freshly ground black pepper
½ teaspoon cayenne
½ teaspoon dried thyme
½ teaspoon dried oregano
1 small bay leaf
4 cups chicken stock
½ pound whole frozen okra, partially thawed, sliced into ½-inch rounds, stem ends discarded
Hot cooked long-grain white rice (page 63)

BROWN FLOUR in ungreased large nonstick skillet over medium-high heat, stirring constantly with wooden spoon and flattening any lumps, for 5 minutes or until deep golden brown. Transfer flour to plate.

Heat oil in large nonstick skillet over medium-high heat. Add sausage and shrimp and cook for 2 minutes or just until shrimp are opaque; remove to plate. Add garlic, white part of green onions, and roasted red peppers and cook for 1 minute or just until tender. Stir in pepper, cayenne, thyme, oregano, and bay leaf. Add browned flour and chicken stock and bring to a boil, stirring constantly. Reduce heat and simmer for 20 minutes or until thickened. Add okra, sausage, and shrimp and cook for 5 minutes or just until heated through. Sprinkle with remaining green onions. Discard bay leaf. Serve in wide, shallow bowls with rice. Serves 2 to 4.

SIDE DISHES & PILAFS

◆ ◆ ◆

Y—

ou may substitute brown rice
for white rice in many of
these recipes. Just remember
that brown rice takes longer
to cook, lends a much earthier taste and
texture and that seasonings may there-
fore have to be adjusted.

BROWN RICE

1 cup long-grain brown rice   1 teaspoon olive oil
2¼ to 2½ cups water   ½ teaspoon salt

BRING RICE, 2¼ cups water, olive oil, and salt to a boil in
heavy medium saucepan over medium-high heat. Cover,
reduce heat to medium-low, and cook for 35 minutes or
until liquid is absorbed and rice is tender (if rice isn't
tender – I like mine a bit chewy – add a few more tablespoons water and continue cooking, covered). Remove
from heat and let stand, uncovered, for 5 minutes before
serving. Makes about 4 cups.

WHITE RICE

1 cup long-grain white rice   ½ teaspoon salt
1¾ cups water

BRING RICE, water, and salt to a boil in heavy medium saucepan over high heat. Reduce heat to medium-low, cover, and cook for 15 minutes or until liquid is absorbed and rice is tender. Remove from heat and let stand, uncovered, for 5 minutes before serving. Serves 2 to 4.

t's difficult to give the exact ratio of rice to water. It depends on the age of the rice (older takes more water) and what size pan is used. Try it as described and if it turns out too firm, add about ¼ cup more water and continue cooking, covered, until tender. ♦ Remember to rinse imported rice, but not domestic rice which has added nutrients. ♦ For 2 cups rice, use 2¾ cups water (serves 4 to 6). For 1½ cups rice, use 2¼ cups water. For 1 cup aged Basmati, use 2 cups water, and for 1 cup Jasmine rice, use 1¾ cups water.

T*wo of my favorite staples –
rice and pasta – combined
into a joyful pairing.*

RICE AND PASTA PILAF

1 tablespoon olive oil
1 cup vermicelli or
   spaghetti, broken into
   ½-inch pieces
1 large garlic clove,
   chopped

1 cup long-grain white rice
2¼ cups chicken stock
½ teaspoon salt

HEAT OIL in heavy medium saucepan over medium-high heat. Add pasta and cook, stirring constantly, for 3 minutes or until golden brown. Add garlic and cook for 1 minute. Add rice and stir. Add chicken stock and salt and bring to a boil. Cover, reduce heat to medium-low, and cook for 15 minutes or until liquid is absorbed and rice is tender. Remove from heat and let stand, uncovered, for 5 minutes before serving. Serves 4 to 6.

COCONUT RICE PILAF

1 cup canned Thai coconut milk	½ teaspoon salt
1 cup water	⅛ teaspoon ground allspice
1 cup long-grain white rice	½ teaspoon Caribbean hot
1 bay leaf	sauce or Tabasco (optional)

BRING COCONUT MILK and water to a boil in heavy medium saucepan over high heat. Add rice, bay leaf, salt, allspice, and hot sauce. Bring back to a boil, cover, reduce heat to medium-low, and cook for 15 minutes or until liquid is absorbed and rice is tender (if rice isn't quite tender, add a little more water and continue cooking, covered). Remove from heat and let stand, uncovered, for 5 minutes before serving. Serves 2 to 4.

R*ice, imbued with rich coconut milk and a hint of allspice, is an excellent accompaniment to Caribbean curries, chicken, fish, or seafood.* ◆ *Canned Thai coconut milk is available in Asian markets.*

Cooking onions until very soft and sweet creates a potent, aromatic addition to rice. ♦ Serve as a side dish to robust-flavored entrées – rich beef stews, grilled steak or chicken and other such earthly delights.

CARAMELIZED ONION PILAF

1 tablespoon olive oil
1 tablespoon butter
1½ cups chopped onion
1 cup long-grain white rice

1¾ cups water
½ teaspoon salt
¼ cup fresh parsley,
   chopped

HEAT OIL and butter in heavy medium saucepan over medium heat. Add onion, reduce heat to medium-low, and cook for 20 minutes or until very tender and golden. Add rice and stir to coat with oil. Raise heat to high, add water and salt, and bring to a boil. Cover, reduce heat to medium-low, and cook for 15 minutes or until liquid is absorbed and rice is tender. Remove from heat and let stand, uncovered, for 5 minutes before serving. Serves 2 to 4.

ROASTED RED PEPPER AND BASIL PILAF

1 tablespoon olive oil
1 large garlic clove,
   chopped
¼ cup chopped onion
⅛ teaspoon cayenne
½ cup homemade or
   bottled roasted red
   peppers, drained,
   coarsely chopped

1 cup long-grain white rice
1¾ cups water
½ teaspoon salt
¼ cup fresh basil leaves,
   chopped

HEAT OIL in heavy medium saucepan over medium-high heat. Add garlic, onion, cayenne, and roasted red peppers and cook for 2 minutes or until tender. Add rice and stir to coat with oil. Add water and salt and bring to a boil. Cover, reduce heat to medium-low, and cook for 15 minutes or until liquid is absorbed and rice is tender. Remove from heat and let stand, uncovered, for 5 minutes before serving. Stir in basil. Serves 4.

R oasted bright red peppers and beautiful fresh basil make rice glisten with the flavors and colors of summer.

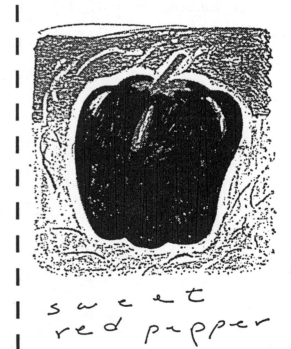

sweet red pepper

This appetizing, classic Southern side dish nick-named "Limping Susan," marries rice with tasty bites of okra flavored with bacon and hot sauce. ◆ Even those who say they don't care for okra, change their minds fast when it's served this way.

OKRA, BACON, AND RICE

4 strips bacon, diced	1 cup long-grain white rice
½ pound frozen whole okra, partially thawed, cut into ½-inch rounds, stem ends discarded	½ teaspoon dried basil
	1¾ cups chicken stock
	½ teaspoon Tabasco
	½ teaspoon salt

COOK BACON until crisp in heavy medium saucepan over medium-high heat. Add okra, rice, and basil and stir to coat with oil. Add chicken stock, Tabasco, and salt and bring to a boil. Cover, reduce heat to medium-low, and cook for 15 minutes or until liquid is absorbed and rice is tender. (If the rice is too *al dente* for your liking, add a little more water and continue cooking, covered.) Remove from heat and let stand, uncovered, for 5 minutes before serving. Serves 4.

PESTO AND PECAN RICE

1 cup long-grain white rice	2 tablespoons pecan halves,
1¾ cups water	toasted, chopped
½ teaspoon salt	Freshly ground black
⅓ cup pesto sauce	pepper

BRING RICE, water, and salt to a boil in heavy medium saucepan over medium-high heat. Cover, reduce heat to medium-low, and cook for 15 minutes or until liquid is absorbed and rice is tender. Remove from heat and let stand, covered, for 5 minutes. Stir in pesto, pecans, and pepper. Serves 4.

here could hardly be a more ravishing addition to rice than fragrant pesto sauce. ◆ To make the exact amount of pesto needed: chop 1 large garlic clove, 1 cup fresh basil leaves, and 2 tablespoons toasted pecans in a food processor; with machine running, add ¼ cup olive oil in a thin stream, then blend in 2 tablespoons grated Parmesan or Romano cheese, salt, and pepper.

RAINBOW FRIED RICE

Rainbow-hued vegetables are tossed with rice for a fresh-tasting Chinese classic. The trick to successful fried rice is to use only cold rice so it doesn't absorb too much oil when fried. ◆ It's best when freshly made, but you can prepare the rice ahead and reheat by adding about 1 tablespoon oil to a heated wok or non-stick skillet, then stir-frying rice just until heated through.

2 tablespoons vegetable oil
2 large eggs, beaten
2 large garlic cloves, chopped
1 tablespoon finely chopped fresh ginger
3 whole green onions, chopped
1 small sweet red pepper, seeded, diced
8 Chinese dried black mushrooms, soaked for 30 minutes in hot water, stems discarded, squeezed dry, thinly sliced

16 snow peas, trimmed, sliced into julienne
½ cup fresh or frozen peas
3 ounces Chinese barbecued pork, cut into strips, or 1 Chinese sausage, steamed, thinly sliced
½ pound cooked small (salad) shrimp
4 cups cold cooked long-grain white rice
½ teaspoon salt
2 tablespoons oyster sauce

HEAT 1 TABLESPOON oil in large nonstick skillet over high heat. Pour in eggs and make a very thin omelet. Transfer to cutting surface and cut into fine strips; set aside.

Heat 1 tablespoon oil in clean pan; when hot, add garlic, ginger, green onions, red pepper, mushrooms, snow peas, and peas. Stir-fry for 1 minute or until heated through. Add pork or sausage and shrimp; toss for 30 seconds. Add rice, breaking up any lumps before adding, and continue stir-frying for 1 minute or until heated through. Stir in egg strips, salt, and oyster sauce until combined. Serves 4 to 6.

SUN-DRIED TOMATO FRIED RICE

1 tablespoon vegetable oil
¼ cup chopped onion
2 large garlic cloves,
    chopped
1 tablespoon finely
    chopped fresh ginger
4 cups cold cooked
    long-grain white rice

½ cup sun-dried tomatoes
    in oil, drained, cut into
    thin strips
Fresh basil leaves,
    shredded for garnish

HEAT OIL in large nonstick skillet over high heat. When hot, add onion, garlic, and ginger; stir fry for 1 minute or until tender. Add rice, breaking up any lumps before adding, and stir for 1 minute or until heated through. Add sun-dried tomatoes, toss, and cook for 1 minute. Garnish with basil. Serves 4.

A charming and unusual tricolor union – Chinese fried rice with Italian sun-dried tomatoes! Sprinkle with fresh basil.

Easy orange-scented rice is great with grilled poultry, fish, and seafood. ♦ *To make lemon pilaf, substitute grated zest of 1 lemon and add 2 tablespoons fresh lemon juice in place of segments.*

ORANGE PILAF

1 tablespoon butter
1 large garlic clove, chopped
1 small onion, chopped
2 teaspoons finely chopped fresh ginger
Grated zest of 1 medium orange

1 cup long-grain white rice
1¾ cups water
½ teaspoon salt
¼ cup chopped orange segments (rind removed)

MELT BUTTER in heavy medium saucepan over medium-high heat. Add garlic, onion, ginger, and half the orange zest; cook for 2 minutes or until tender. Add rice and stir to coat with oil. Add water and salt and bring to a boil. Cover, reduce heat to medium-low, and cook for 15 minutes or until liquid is absorbed and rice is tender. Stir in orange segments. Remove from heat and let stand, uncovered, for 5 minutes, then stir in remaining orange zest. Serves 2 to 4.

BAKED RICE WITH CHEESE AND CHILES

2 tablespoons butter
2 large garlic cloves, chopped
1 small onion, finely chopped
1 cup Basmati, rinsed, or long-grain white rice
2 cups water
½ teaspoon salt

½ cup sour cream
¼ cup chopped fresh cilantro
½ cup pickled sliced jalapeños, drained, coarsely chopped
1 cup grated Monterey Jack cheese

ot and spicy, I've included this yummy, cheesy Mexican rice dish from my book All the Best Mexican Meals because it's simply superlative.

MELT BUTTER in heavy medium saucepan over medium-high heat. Add garlic and onion and cook for 2 minutes or until tender. Stir in rice, add water (if using long-grain, use ¼ cup less water) and salt, and bring to a boil. Cover, reduce heat to medium-low, and cook for 20 minutes or until liquid is absorbed and rice is tender. Transfer rice to a lightly greased 8-inch square glass baking dish and allow to cool thoroughly.

Preheat oven to 425°F.

Stir in sour cream and cilantro until combined, then stir in chiles and grated cheese. Bake, uncovered, for 20 minutes or until heated through and lightly flecked with golden brown. Do not overcook. Serves 4.

Rice lends itself to myriad flavorings. ◆ The simple addition of chopped scallions (commonly known as green onions) gives attractive flecks of green and a very delicate hint of onion.

SCALLION RICE PILAF

1 tablespoon olive oil	½ teaspoon salt
1 large garlic clove, chopped	1 tablespoon butter
1 cup long-grain white rice	3 whole green onions, chopped
1¾ cups water	

HEAT OIL in heavy medium saucepan over medium-high heat. Add garlic and cook for 1 minute or until tender. Add rice and stir to coat with oil. Add water and salt and bring to a boil. Cover, reduce heat to medium-low, and cook for 15 minutes or until liquid is absorbed and rice is tender.

Melt butter in small skillet over medium-high heat. Add green onions and cook for 1 minute or just until tender. Stir into rice and serve. Serves 2 to 4.

RICE WITH FETA, MINT, OLIVES, AND TOMATOES

1 cup long-grain white rice
1¾ cups water
½ teaspoon salt
½ cup crumbled feta cheese
1 green onion (green part only), chopped
1 tablespoon chopped fresh mint leaves

1 ripe medium tomato, coarsely diced
6 Greek black olives (Kalamata), pitted, cut into strips

*L*ots of verve! ♦ *Rice is boldly awakened with pungent Greek feta cheese and olives, refreshing mint, and fresh ripe tomatoes.*

BRING RICE, water, and salt to a boil in heavy medium saucepan over high heat. Cover, reduce heat to medium-low, and cook for 15 minutes or until liquid is absorbed and rice is tender. Stir in cheese, green onion, mint, tomato, and olives. Remove from heat and let stand, uncovered, for 5 minutes before serving. Serves 2 to 4.

BLACK olives

Fragrant Basmati rice, pepped-up with shreds of ginger and slivers of garlic, offers a spirited accompaniment to any number of curries, poultry, or fish entrées. ◆ Don't make this with regular long-grain rice, only Basmati will do.

GINGER AND GARLIC RICE

1 tablespoon vegetable oil
5 very thin quarter-size slices fresh ginger, very finely shredded
4 large garlic cloves, sliced into slivers

1 cup Basmati rice, rinsed
2 cups water
½ teaspoon salt
¼ teaspoon hot red pepper flakes (optional)

HEAT OIL in heavy medium saucepan over medium-high heat. Add ginger and garlic and cook for 1 minute or until tender. Add rice and stir to coat with oil. Add water, salt, and red pepper flakes. Bring to a boil, cover, reduce heat to medium-low, and cook, stirring occasionally, for 20 minutes or until liquid is absorbed and rice is tender. Serves 4.

WILD RICE AND LEEKS

¼ cup (½ stick) butter
1¼ cups chopped white
   part of leeks (well rinsed)
½ pound wild rice (about
   1⅓ cups)

1½ cups chicken stock
½ cup French dry white
   vermouth

MELT BUTTER in heavy medium saucepan over medium-high heat. Add leeks and cook for 4 minutes or until tender. Add rice and stir to combine. Pour in chicken stock and vermouth. Bring to a rapid boil over high heat, cover, then take off heat. Let stand for 1 hour.

Bring rice back to a boil. Cover, reduce heat to medium-low, and cook for 35 minutes or until rice is tender, but still chewy, and liquid is absorbed, stirring occasionally. Serves 6.

Wild, woodsy-flavored rice is one of my favorite companions to Thanksgiving and Christmas turkey. But it's also perfect with any roasted game or poultry. ◆ For a change of pace, replace the leeks with a chopped large garlic clove, a chopped medium-small onion, and ½ pound coarsely chopped mushrooms.

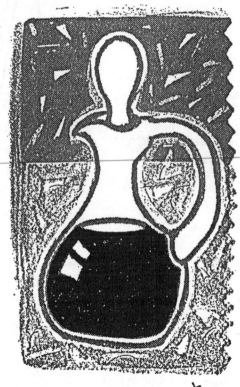

cruet

SALADS

♦ ♦ ♦

L eftover rice, teamed with tangy tomatoes, artichokes, capers, and roasted peppers, all accented with lemon, turns into a terrific salad to serve alongside grilled fish, seafood, or poultry.

ARTICHOKE, TOMATO, AND LEMON RICE SALAD

3 cups cooked long-grain white rice, at room temperature
1 whole green onion, chopped
1 ripe medium tomato, coarsely chopped
6-ounce jar marinated artichokes, drained, coarsely chopped
2 tablespoons capers, drained
¼ cup homemade or bottled roasted red peppers, drained, chopped

Freshly ground black pepper
Grated zest of 1 medium lemon
2 tablespoons olive oil
2 tablespoons fresh lemon juice
1 teaspoon Dijon mustard
2 tablespoons finely chopped fresh flat-leaf parsley
Salt

COMBINE RICE, green onion, tomato, artichokes, capers, roasted red peppers, pepper, and lemon zest in bowl and stir gently to combine.

Whisk oil, lemon juice, and mustard until thickened, pour over rice mixture, and toss to blend. Add parsley and salt and stir to combine. Adjust seasoning and serve at room temperature. Serves 4 to 6.

TOMATO, MUSHROOM, AND RICE SALAD

1½ cups long-grain white rice
2¼ cups water
½ teaspoon salt
2 ripe medium tomatoes, coarsely diced
½ pound white mushrooms, wiped clean, thinly sliced
2 whole green onions, chopped

Salt
Freshly ground black pepper
¼ cup olive oil
2 tablespoons red wine vinegar
1 to 2 tablespoons dried tarragon

BRING RICE, water, and salt to a boil in heavy medium saucepan over high heat. Cover, reduce heat to medium-low, and cook for 20 minutes or until liquid is absorbed and rice is tender. Cool to room temperature.

Combine rice, tomatoes, mushrooms, green onions, salt, and pepper in large bowl. Whisk oil and vinegar until thickened, pour over rice mixture, and toss to blend. Add tarragon to taste. Adjust seasoning and serve at room temperature. Serves 4 to 6.

Light and refreshing, this marvelous mushroom salad is easily totable and makes a nice alternative to serve with grilled fish or chicken or other barbecue fare.

*Q*uite lively and pungent with summery sun-dried tomatoes and perky black olives. Feel free to use fewer than I've suggested, if you prefer a more low-key rendition.

WILD RICE SALAD WITH SUN-DRIED TOMATOES AND OLIVES

1 cup wild rice
2 cups water
¾ cup homemade or bottled roasted red peppers, drained, coarsely chopped
20 large sun-dried tomato halves in oil, drained, coarsely diced
1 cup Greek black olives (Kalamata), pitted, cut into strips

¾ cup fresh basil leaves, chopped
¼ cup olive oil
2 tablespoons fresh lemon juice
Salt
Freshly ground black pepper

BRING RICE and water to a boil in heavy medium saucepan over high heat. Cover, reduce heat to medium-low, and cook for 35 minutes or until rice is tender but still chewy. Transfer to large bowl and allow to cool to room temperature. Stir in roasted red peppers, sun-dried tomatoes, olives, basil, oil, lemon juice, salt, and pepper until combined. Serve at room temperature. Serves 6 to 8.

WILD AND BASMATI RICE SALAD WITH TOASTED COCONUT, CURRANTS, AND PECANS

1 cup wild rice
2 cups water
1 cup Basmati rice, rinsed
2 cups water
Grated zest of 1 large orange
2 green onions (green part only), chopped
¾ cup dried currants
3 tablespoons desiccated coconut, toasted

¼ cup pecan halves, toasted
¼ cup olive oil
1½ teaspoons Dijon mustard
2 tablespoons tarragon vinegar
1 to 2 tablespoons dried tarragon
Salt

BRING WILD RICE and 2 cups water to a boil in medium saucepan. Cover, reduce heat to medium-low, and cook for 35 minutes or until tender, but still chewy. In second saucepan, bring Basmati rice and 2 cups water to a boil. Cover, reduce heat to medium-low, and cook for 15 minutes or until tender. Cool wild and Basmati rice to room temperature.

Combine wild and Basmati rice, orange zest, green onions, currants, coconut, and pecans in large bowl.

Whisk oil, mustard, vinegar, and tarragon to taste in small bowl until thickened. Drizzle over salad, toss gently, and season with salt. Serve at room temperature or chilled. Serves 4 to 6.

Basmati and wild rice, bathed in a tarragon dressing and sweetly seasoned with orange zest, toasted coconut, and pecans, looks as great as it tastes. ◆ This is a variation on a recipe from my book, All The Best Salads.

An outrageously pretty salad for a porch lunch on a hot summer day. ◆ This is a taste-as-you-go salad since the flavor depends on what flowers and herbs are used. ◆ Be sure to use only organic, edible flowers – some are poisonous – not ones from florists or garden centers which have been sprayed with insecticides. ◆ Only the petals are edible, not the pistils, stamens, stems, and leaves. The more color combinations, the more beautiful the salad. Choose from roses, pansies, Johnny-jump-ups, chrysanthemums, nasturtiums (both leaves and flowers are edible), and herb flowers such as chive blossoms, thyme flowers, and basil flowers. ◆ Use scissors to snip large petals into julienne.

FLOWER PETALS AND RICE SALAD

2 tablespoons olive oil
1 tablespoon fresh lemon
   juice
1 teaspoon Dijon mustard
Salt
Freshly ground black
   pepper
4 cups cooked long-grain
   white rice, at room
   temperature

About ½ cup mixed edible
   flowers, julienned, plus
   extra for garnish
Snipped mixed fresh herbs:
   dill, chives, chervil,
   tarragon

WHISK OLIVE OIL, lemon juice, mustard, salt, and pepper in small bowl until thickened. Stir rice and dressing in large bowl until combined. Sprinkle with flowers and herbs and toss again. Taste and adjust seasoning and garnish with flowers. Serve at once. Serves 4.

DESSERTS

◆ ◆ ◆

From my book, All The Best Muffins and Quick Breads, *these earthy muffins make a terrific nibble, or serve* them with poultry, game, or an assertive salad. ♦ *You may also make them with 1½ cups leftover cooked cold, wild rice and skip the first step.*

WILD RICE AND SHIITAKE MUFFINS

1½ cups chicken stock
¾ cup wild rice
¼ cup (½ stick) butter
1 small onion, chopped
1 small garlic clove, chopped
6 ounces fresh shiitake mushrooms, stems discarded, very coarsely chopped

1½ cups all-purpose flour
1 tablespoon sugar
1 tablespoon baking powder
½ teaspoon salt
2 large eggs
1 cup milk

BRING CHICKEN STOCK and rice to a boil in small heavy saucepan over high heat. Cover, reduce heat, and cook for 45 minutes or until liquid is absorbed and rice is tender, but still chewy (add more liquid if necessary). Set aside to cool completely.

Melt butter in medium nonstick skillet over medium-high heat. Add onion and garlic and cook for 2 minutes or until tender. Add mushrooms and cook for 2 minutes or just until cooked through; set aside to cool.

Preheat oven to 400°F, adjust oven rack to top third position, and coat 12-cup muffin pan with vegetable spray.

Combine flour, sugar, baking powder, and salt in large bowl. Whisk eggs and milk in medium bowl; stir in cooled rice and mushroom mixture. Pour liquid mixture over dry ingredients and fold in with rubber spatula just until combined; do not overmix.

Spoon batter into prepared muffin cups, dividing evenly. Bake for 20 minutes or until tester comes out clean. Turn out onto rack and serve warm. Makes 12 muffins.

SHORTBREAD COOKIES

½ cup (1 stick) butter, at room temperature
⅓ cup sugar
1 teaspoon vanilla

¾ cup all-purpose flour
¼ cup rice flour
Pinch salt

PREHEAT OVEN to 325°F.

Cream butter, sugar, and vanilla in bowl of electric mixer. Add all-purpose and rice flours and salt and blend just until combined. Press dough firmly into 9-inch glass pie plate. Bake for 30 to 40 minutes or until golden. Remove pan to wire rack, immediately cut into 8 wedges (but don't remove from pan) and, using tines of fork, pierce each wedge all the way through in 3 places to make a pattern. Cool completely. Makes 8 cookies.

R*ice flour, added to all-purpose flour, makes an extra-short shortbread. ♦ Rice flour is available at most super-markets, specialty and health food stores.*

butter

A wild – and not-quite-like-Mommy-used-to-make-it – version of everyone's basic comfort food. ♦ To cook rice, see Wild Rice and Basmati Rice Salad with Toasted Coconut, Currants, and Pecans (page 83).

WILD RICE PUDDING

2 cups cooked wild rice	½ teaspoon salt
3 cups milk (not low fat)	¼ teaspoon grated nutmeg
1 cup heavy cream	¼ cup dark raisins
½ cup sugar	¼ cup golden raisins
2 teaspoons vanilla	Cream for serving

PREHEAT OVEN to 350°F.

Combine cooked wild rice, milk, cream, sugar, vanilla, salt, nutmeg, and raisins in shallow 1½-quart baking dish. Bake, uncovered, for 1 hour and 20 minutes or until set at the edges but still creamy inside; do not overcook. Serve warm, with a little cream drizzled over, if you like. Serves 6.

CITRUS-SCENTED RICE PUDDING

½ cup long-grain white rice
Grated zest of 1 medium
  lemon
Grated zest of 1 medium
  orange
¼ cup sugar
3 cups milk (not low fat)
1 cup heavy cream

1 tablespoon vanilla
½ teaspoon grated nutmeg
½ teaspoon ground
  cinnamon
¼ teaspoon salt
½ cup golden raisins
Heavy cream for serving
  (optional)

PREHEAT OVEN to 350°F.

Combine rice, lemon zest, orange zest, sugar, milk, heavy cream, vanilla, nutmeg, cinnamon, salt, and raisins in a shallow 1½-quart baking dish. Bake, uncovered, for 1 hour and 20 minutes or until set at the edges but still creamy inside; do not overcook. Serve warm from the oven, at room temperature, or chilled with a drizzle cream if desired. Serves 6.

Scented with lemon, orange, cinnamon, and nutmeg, this peerless pudding has the added bonus of perfuming the kitchen with its alluring aroma while it's baking.

R *ice pudding for chocoholics. To carry the indulgence that extra step, serve with sweetened fresh sliced berries and whipped cream.* ♦ *Best if served fresh and warm from the oven (and that way, you don't have to wait!).*

CHOCOLATE RICE PUDDING

½ cup long-grain white rice	2 teaspoons vanilla
¼ cup plus 2 tablespoons sugar	½ teaspoon ground cinnamon
3 ounces semisweet chocolate, coarsely chopped	¼ teaspoon salt
	3 cups milk (not low fat)
½ cup currants	1 cup heavy cream
Grated zest of 1 medium orange	Cream for serving

PREHEAT OVEN to 350°F.

Combine rice, sugar, chocolate, currants, orange zest, vanilla, cinnamon, salt, milk, and heavy cream in shallow 1½-quart baking dish. Bake, uncovered, for 1 hour and 20 minutes or until set at the edges but still creamy inside. Serve warm with a drizzle of cream if desired. Serves 6.

INDEX

◆ ◆ ◆

Books in Joie Warner's ALL THE BEST series

Available from

HEARST/WILLIAM MORROW

Books in Joie Warner's ALL THE BEST series

— also available —

Available from
HEARST/WILLIAM MORROW